Thinking.

Loving.

Doing.

OTHER CROSSWAY BOOKS:

Thinking.

Loving.

Doing.

GENERAL EDITORS

JOHN PIPER
& DAVID MATHIS

CONTRIBUTIONS BY
Rick Warren | Francis Chan | R. Albert Mohler Jr.
R. C. Sproul | Thabiti Anyabwile

:: CROSSWAY

WHEATON, ILLINOIS

Library of Congress Cataloging-in-Publication Data

Thinking. loving. doing.: a call to glorify God with heart and mind / John Piper and David Mathis, general editors ; contributors, Rick Warren . . . [et al.].
    p. cm.
    Proceedings of a conference.
    Includes bibliographical references and indexes.
    ISBN 978-1-4335-2651-0 (tp)
    1. Thought and thinking—Religious aspects—Christianity—Congresses. 2. Love—Religious aspects—Christianity—Congresses. 3. God (Christianity)—Worship and love—Congresses. 4. Christian life—Congresses. I. Piper, John, 1946-   . II. Mathis, David, 1980-   . III. Warren, Richard, 1954-   . IV. Title.
BV4598.4.T45   2011
248—dc22   2011012815

To
JOHN FRAME and VERN POYTHRESS
who have taught us so well
through the life of the mind
not to neglect our hearts
or our hands

Contents

Contributors

Thabiti Anyabwile is senior pastor of First Baptist Church of Grand Cayman, Cayman Islands, and served previously at Capitol Hill Baptist Church in Washington DC. He is married to Kristie, and they have three children (Afiya, Eden, and Titus). He blogs at *Pure Church* at The Gospel Coalition website and is the author of *The Gospel for Muslims: An Encouragement to Share Christ with Confidence*.

Francis Chan founded Cornerstone Church in Simi Valley, California, where he was the primary preacher/teacher for sixteen years and also established Eternity Bible College. Francis is the author of the best-selling book *Crazy Love: Overwhelmed by a Relentless God*. He and his wife, Lisa, have four children (Rachel, Mercy, Eliana, and Ezekiel) and now live in San Francisco, California.

David Mathis is an elder at Bethlehem Baptist Church in Minneapolis, Minnesota, and executive pastoral assistant to John Piper. He is coeditor of *With Calvin in the Theater of God: The Glory of Christ and Everyday Life*, as well as *The Pastor as Scholar and the Scholar as Pastor: Reflections on Life and Ministry*. He and his wife, Megan, have twin sons, Carson and Coleman.

R. Albert Mohler Jr. is the ninth president of The Southern Baptist Theological Seminary in Louisville, Kentucky, and keeps a blog with regular commentary on moral, cultural, and theological issues at albertmohler.com. He is the author of several books, and he and his wife, Mary, have two children.

John Piper is pastor for preaching and vision at Bethlehem Baptist Church in Minneapolis, Minnesota, where he has served since 1980. He has written over forty books, including *Desiring God*; *The Pleasures of God*; *Don't Waste Your Life*; *Seeing and Savoring Jesus Christ*; *God Is the Gospel*; *Think*; and most recently *Bloodlines*. John and his wife, Noël, have five children and an increasing number of grandchildren.

R. C. Sproul is founder of Ligonier Ministries, chancellor of Ligonier Academy of Biblical and Theological Studies, executive editor of *Tabletalk* magazine, and teacher and host of the daily radio program *Renewing Your Mind*. He is senior minister of preaching and teaching at St. Andrews Chapel in Sanford, Florida, and author of more than seventy books, including classics *The Holiness of God* and *Chosen by God*. He and his wife, Vesta, have two grown children.

Rick Warren is founding pastor of Saddleback Church in Lake Forest, California. He has a worldwide influence on the topics of leadership development, poverty, health, education, and faith and culture, and is known as a global strategist and committed philanthropist. Rick is author of *The Purpose-Driven Life*, and he and Kay, his wife of over thirty years, have three adult children (Amy, Josh, and Matthew) and four grandchildren.

Introduction

Think, Love, Do: In Gospel Perspective

DAVID MATHIS

The gospel has instincts. Part and parcel of the central Christian message is an impulse toward purity and an impulse toward unity. The purity instinct resists the compromise of the message, while the unity instinct is eager to link arms with others also celebrating the biblical gospel.

The reason purity and unity are, in this way, "built into" the gospel is that the God of the gospel is himself both a purifier and a unifier. No one cares more for the purity of the gospel—that his central message to humanity not be altered or tainted—than God himself. And, mark this, no one cares more for the unity of his church around her Savior, his own Son, than God himself. God is the great purifier and unifier.

So likewise, his gospel—which not only saves and sanctifies but is the richest, deepest, and fullest revelation of who God is—has both a purity impulse and a unity impulse "pre-packaged" into it, as it were. It's quite simple on paper and gets terribly messy in real life.

How We Mess It Up

For those of us living this side of the fall as well as this side of heaven—sinners all but one—our purity and unity antennae inevitably function improperly. Some of us have lost the purity impulse altogether. We are happy to say things easy to hear and hard to misinterpret, but none of the tough stuff. We are eager to bring people together—the more the merrier—but we have lost spine enough to speak the difficult, potentially relationship-threatening truths like our Savior does.

On the other hand, many of us—perhaps an inordinate number in the Reformed-evangelical community of which I am a part—have repressed the unity impulse. We can spot a supposed theological error from a mile away, and we have no trouble spinning out immediate shaming (and sassy) responses and calculated separations. Anyone different from us, in just about any way, could be a candidate for a verbal beat-down, or at least a relational snub. We have lost the heart to love like our Savior does.

And a third type creeps in among us reckless sinners: those of us inconsistent enough to swing back and forth between both mistakes, sometimes purifying with no concern for gospel unity, other times uniting without a care for gospel purity. We speak the truth without loving on Monday and love without speaking the truth on Tuesday— all the while falling short of Paul's simple but nearly impossible challenge for "speaking the truth in love" (Eph. 4:15).

The Good and Bad of "Unifiers and Purifiers"[1]

The purifiers among us may thrive on "watch[ing] out for those who cause divisions and create obstacles contrary to the doctrine that you have been taught"—and then excel at Paul's next charge, "avoid them" (Rom. 16:17), but only after really dishing it out in person, or even better, behind the fortress of electronic communication. We

---

[1]"Unifiers and Purifiers" is the title of a blog post by Kevin DeYoung available at http://thegospelcoalition.org/blogs/kevindeyoung/2011/01/20/. He quotes J. Robertson McQuilken in his explanation of the tension between purifying discipline (or faithfulness) and unifying forgiveness (or love):

There is a great polarization between the professional unifiers on the one hand and the professional purifiers on the other. It seems that a person must work at uniting all churches no matter how delinquent in doctrine or life or that he must give himself wholly to separating all the wheat from the tares now. . . . [But] Imbalance does not come from an overemphasis. It is impossible to have too much love or too much faithfulness. However, it is quite possible to have unfaithfulness masquerading as love. When God's people compromise through sentimentality or self-love or for some other reason are unwilling to exercise church discipline, they are unfaithful though they speak much of love. Again, it is quite possible to have unlove masquerading as faithfulness. When God's people create schism by disciplining the wrong person, or with the wrong motive, or in the wrong way, they are unloving though they speak much of faithfulness. I do not ask the ecumenist to be less loving. I urge him to be more faithful. I do not ask the separatist to be less faithful. I urge him to be more loving. ("Whatever Happened to Church Discipline?" *Christianity Today*, March 29, 1974, 8.)

DeYoung comments, "The true Christian will not pit grace against truth, love against faithfulness, discipline against forgiveness, unity against purity. But neither do we want the fullness of one half of the pair to be an excuse for a deficiency on the other side."

might be eager to identify "a person who stirs up division" and may be even more eager to "have nothing more to do with him" (Titus 3:10). Some all-or-nothing purifiers are so focused on sniffing out the errors of other Christians that they don't seem to pause long enough to consider whether they themselves are the ones causing the very divisions Paul is warning against. There is a beauty in the purity instinct, the beauty of preserving the gospel, but for us sinners a cluster of dangers can accompany it—arrogance, hatred, meanness, malice, slander.

The unifiers, on the other hand, glory in "how good and pleasant it is when brothers dwell in unity!" (Ps. 133:1) and remind us that Jesus prayed in John 17 that we "may become perfectly one, so that the world may know" (v. 23). The unifiers are eager to say with Paul, "May the God of endurance and encouragement grant you to live in such harmony with one another, in accord with Christ Jesus, that together you may with one voice glorify the God and Father of our Lord Jesus Christ" (Rom. 15:5–6). It's the oneness texts that float the unifying boat—especially Ephesians 4:

> [Be] eager to maintain the unity of the Spirit in the bond of peace. There is one body and one Spirit—just as you were called to the one hope that belongs to your call—one Lord, one faith, one baptism, one God and Father of all, who is over all and through all and in all. . . .
>
> And he gave the apostles, the prophets, the evangelists, the shepherds and teachers, to equip the saints for the work of ministry, for building up the body of Christ, until we all attain to the unity of the faith and of the knowledge of the Son of God, to mature manhood, to the measure of the stature of the fullness of Christ, so that we may no longer be children, tossed to and fro by the waves and carried about by every wind of doctrine, by human cunning, by craftiness in deceitful schemes. Rather, speaking the truth in love, we are to grow up in every way into him who is the head, into Christ, from whom the whole body, joined and held together by every joint with which it is equipped, when each part is working properly, makes the body grow so that it builds itself up in love. (vv. 3–6, 11–16)

Is there ever beauty in Christian unity! And yet the cluster of dangers, due to our sin, that can attach to it include cowardice, practical-philosophical apathy, and doctrinal indifference.

Challenged in the Context of Community

One reality that helps us check our frequent blind spots and mis-judgments is Christian community. God rarely leaves us without a communal context in which some biblical purity and unity are simul-taneously functioning in small measure (or we wouldn't have a com-munity), hopefully guiding us in such decisions. Those of us with an acute bent for purity need to hear often from the unifiers, and those of us typically leaning toward unity need the regular perspective of the purifiers.

As our finitude conspires with our sin, none of us sees any piece of reality from every perspective (as God does), and what we do see, we frequently misappropriate. So we benefit incalculably to know well the perspectives of others and run them through our developing grid of Bible-informed and Spirit-indwelt thinking, loving, and doing.

Profiting from Multiple Perspectives

John Frame and Vern Poythress (to whom this book is dedicated) have been as helpful as any in leading Christians (particularly Reformed evangelicals) to understand our need for viewing reality from multiple perspectives. Frame writes:

> Because we are not God, because we are finite, not infinite, we can-not know everything at a glance, and therefore our knowledge is limited to one perspective or another.
>
> God knows absolutely everything, because he planned ev-erything, made everything, and determines what happens in the world he made. So we describe him as omniscient. One interesting implication of God's omniscience is that he not only knows all the facts about himself and the world; he also knows how everything appears from every possible perspective. . . . God's knowledge, then, is not only omniscient, but omniperspectival. He knows from his own infinite perspective; but that infinite perspective includes a knowledge of all created perspectives, possible and actual.
>
> But we are different. We are finite, and our knowledge is fi-nite. I can only know the world from the limited perspective of my own body and mind. The effects of this finitude, and even more of sin, should caution us against cocksureness in our claims to knowl-edge. I am not saying that we should doubt everything. Certainly

my limited perspective gives me no excuse to doubt that I have five fingers, or that 2+2 = 4, or that God exists. Our finitude does not imply that all our knowledge is erroneous, or that certainty is impossible. But we do, in most situations, need to guard against mistakes.

One way to increase our knowledge and our level of certainty is by supplementing our own perspectives with those of others. When our own resources fail us, we can consult friends, authorities, books, etc. We can travel to other places, visit people of other cultures. Even to get a good understanding of a tree, we need to walk around it, look at it from many angles.[2]

The unifiers need the purifiers, and vice versa. And not unrelated is the thinking-loving-doing triad we are developing in this book. As Scripture makes plain, the Christian life is a multidimensional reality. The life-of-the-mind perspective alone won't capture the full biblical texture. The Christian life is more than mere intellect. And the angle of feeling—the life of the heart—won't do justice by itself to the full biblical witness. It's more than simply passion. And doing isn't the alone biblical perspective on the Christian life. More is happening than mere deeds. Rather, holistic Christian existence is irreducibly thinking, loving, and doing—mind, heart, and hands.

The Importance of Thinking

Healthy Christianity clearly appreciates the life of the mind. Love God *"with all your mind,"* says Jesus (Matt. 22:37). "Think over what I say," Paul tells Timothy, and us with him (2 Tim. 2:7). When Proverbs instructs us to "seek it like silver," the referent is insight, understanding, and the knowledge of God (Prov. 2:3–5).[3] It is a tragedy that in many Christian circles, the life of the mind is not prized, and it is even diminished. Anti-intellectualism in the church (of all places!) is a calamity given that Christians this side of heaven are people of a Book, and thus irreducibly thinkers in some sense.

Jewish author and talk-show host Dennis Prager observes:

---

[2]John M. Frame, "A Primer on Perspectivalism," rev. ed., available at http://www.frame-poythress.org/frame_articles/2008Primer.htm.

[3]For more on these texts and the life of the Christian mind, see John Piper, *Think: The Life of the Mind and the Love of God* (Wheaton, IL: Crossway, 2010). As we will say again below, this book was the inspiration for the conference that birthed these chapters on thinking, loving, and doing.

One thing I noticed about evangelicals is that they do not read.
They do not read the Bible, they do not read the great Christian
thinkers, they have never heard of Aquinas. If they are Presbyterian, they've never read the founders of Presbyterianism. I do not
understand that. As a Jew, that's confusing to me. The commandment of study is so deep in Judaism that we immerse ourselves
in study. God gave us a brain; aren't we to use it in His service?
When I walk into an Evangelical Christian's home and see a total
of 30 books, most of them best sellers, I do not understand. I have
bookcases of Christian books, and I am a Jew. Why do I have more
Christian books than 98 percent of the Christians in America?
That is so bizarre to me.[4]

This hits close to home. Honestly, such an evangelical allergy to
books, and its accompanying subtle form of anti-intellectualism,
characterized what I would have called "my Christian walk" in high
school. I hated reading. Today at my parents' home in Spartanburg,
South Carolina, in my old room (now the guestroom) lies a thick stack
of CliffsNotes that reminds me how I cut corners to make it through
high school reading assignments. At the time, I would not have ver-
balized any formal anti-intellectual opinions, but my disdain for reading was eroding the foundation of my present and future thinking.
Though many tremendous gospel seeds were sewn in those years, it
now seems that it was my freshman year in college when God really
turned on the lights of new birth, and with it came a voracious appe-
tite for reading—and in its wake, a more engaged life of the mind.[5]

The Limits of Thinking

So thinking (and its companion, reading, especially God's Book) is
essential to normal, healthy Christianity. But growth in knowledge
is only one aspect of our sanctification, not the whole. Here again it
helps to recognize that reality is multidimensional. An important
facet of Christian growth, no doubt, comes in the realm of the mind.
But sanctification happens in its fullest in everyday life, not merely

---

[4]Dennis Prager, "A Civilization That Believes in Nothing," *The Door* (November/December 1990), 15.
Thanks to Justin Taylor for pointing me to this quote.
[5]For more on the roots of and remedy to Christian anti-intellectualism, see "Facing the Challenge of Anti-
Intellectualism" in Piper, *Think*, pp. 117–54.

through hearing lectures in classrooms and reading books at desks.[6] What of the heart?

The Importance and Limits of Feeling

Christianity is also plainly about feeling. The heart is central. Our faith is irreducibly emotional. "You shall love the Lord your God *with all your heart,*" Jesus says (Matt. 22:37). God cares immensely about our hearts—and about being the one who captures them. Some of his first diagnoses of humanity's post-fall condition is that "every intention of the thoughts of his heart was only evil continually" (Gen. 6:5) and "the intention of man's heart is evil from his youth" (Gen. 8:21). Sinners have not only the obstacle of "the futility of their minds . . . [being] darkened in their understanding, alienated from the life of God because of the ignorance that is in them," but more deeply, Paul writes, humanity's flawed thinking is "due to their hardness of heart" (Eph. 4:17–18).

And so God's redeeming inclinations include his desire to have his people "search after him with all your heart" (Deut. 4:29) and "serve the LORD your God with joyfulness and gladness of heart" (Deut. 28:47). Proverbs tells us, "Keep your heart with all vigilance, for from it flow the springs of life" (Prov. 4:23). Paul says he wants the Roman believers (and us) to "become obedient from the heart" (Rom. 6:17). God does not circumvent the heart in producing true gospel obedience and advance.

Yet there is more to sanctification than mere feeling, central as the affections are. Paul is pained when he sees in his Jewish kinsmen "a zeal for God, but not according to knowledge" (Rom. 10:2). And the "thinking texts" mentioned above conspire with a litany of others to teach us that growth in godliness is more than just feeling. And what of the significance of doing?

The Importance and Limits of Doing

Christianity is indeed about doing. Likely most memorable in this regard is James's charge, "Be doers of the word, and not hearers only,

---

[6]Perhaps as an overreaction to anti-intellectualism, unfortunately, there is a subtle but pervasive assumption in some churches and ministries that sanctification comes only (or mainly) through education and advancing the mind.

deceiving yourselves" (James 1:22). God has saved us not merely for right thinking and deep feeling but "for good works, which God prepared beforehand, that we should walk in them" (Eph. 2:10). The God who made this physical world means for what we think and feel about him to come to expression in the lived-out actions of worship, witness, and practical deeds of love. Doing counts big time.

But we have seen from Scripture's clarion calls to thinking and loving that the Christian life isn't mere doing. Again, the full-orbed Christian existence is multidimensional. We are summoned to think and love and do, all to the glory of God in Christ, and not diminish any of the three.

We Need Each Other

We travel some varying terrain in our journeys to be "conformed to the image of" Jesus (Rom. 8:29). With the Spirit's help in both redeeming our natural giftings and creating new strengths in union with Christ, some of us sprout quickly with regard to the mind, or the heart, or practical life skills (the hands), or some combination of the three. Rarely do we stay balanced in our growth. Typically one aspect, or two combined, see advance while one or two lag behind. And this happens not only on the personal level but also on the corporate, in the varying pockets of the faith.

New York pastor Tim Keller, himself Reformed (which many might see as the thinking branch of Christianity), writes the following after speaking at a Willow Creek Leadership Summit (which many might see as part of the doing branch). Roughly analogous to our thinking-loving-doing triad is his prophet-priest-king terminology:

> The time at Willow led me to reflect on how much criticism this church has taken over the years. On the one hand, my own "camp"—the non-mainline Reformed world—has been critical of its pragmatism, its lack of emphasis on sound doctrine. On the other hand, the emerging and post-modern ministries and leaders have disdained Willow's individualism, its program-centered, "corporate" ethos. These critiques, I think, are partly right, but when you are actually there you realize many of the most negative evaluations are caricatures.

John Frame's "tri-perspectivalism" helps me understand Willow. The Willow Creek style churches have a "kingly" emphasis on leadership, strategic thinking, and wise administration. The danger there is that the mechanical obscures how organic and spontaneous church life can be. The Reformed churches have a "prophetic" emphasis on preaching, teaching, and doctrine. The danger there is that we can have a naïve and unBiblical view that, if we just expound the Word faithfully, everything else in the church—leader development, community building, stewardship of resources, unified vision—will just happen by themselves. The emerging churches have a "priestly" emphasis on community, liturgy and sacraments, service and justice. The danger there is to view "community" as the magic bullet in the same way Reformed people view preaching.

By thinking in this way, it makes it possible for me to love and appreciate the best representatives of each of these contemporary evangelical "traditions."[7]

In our scheme, the "thinkers" (mind) would be the Reformed; the "feelers" (heart), the massive swaths of Pentecostal and charismatic networks (either in addition to, or perhaps rather than, the now greatly diminishing number of those labeling themselves "emerging"); and the "doers" (hands), the more practically oriented "leadership" segments of the church, like Willow. And the point is that none of us gets it all right. Those truly born again, and united to Jesus by faith, need each other. The thinkers need the feelers and the doers—individually and corporately. The feelers need the thinkers and doers. The doers, the feelers and thinkers. And coming full circle, the purifiers need the unifiers—and the unifiers the purifiers.

A Challenge to the Reformed

My own sphere is the broader evangelical Reformed community, and the majority of this volume's contributors hail from that network. And likely many readers of this book consider themselves either broadly or more narrowly Reformed, at least theologically. So we may do well here to pause just briefly and challenge the home team.[8]

---

[7]Tim Keller, "The 'Kingly' Willow Creek Conference," posted Sept. 30, 2009, at http://redeemercitytocity. com/blog/view.jsp?Blog_param=44.

[8]For those readers identifying more with the Pentecostal, charismatic, emerging, "leadership," or other segments of the church, maybe this short section of Reformed self-critique can serve as a model for you to evaluate the strengths and weaknesses of your community.

In his article "Machen's Warrior Children," Frame observes, "Reformed churches tend to glory in their distinctives: their history, their ethnic origins, the theological battles of the past that have made them different from others."[9] He is quick to note, "Not every theological difference, of course, is a difference of perspective. Sometimes one must simply choose one view that is true and another that is false." But far too often, he laments, "perspectival differences enter into the nature of the disagreement" between Christians.[10] We have a penchant for dividing over things we shouldn't.

Room for Reformed Growth

This side of heaven, no sector of the church has "arrived." Some pockets, in sweepingly general terms, seem characterized by better thinkers, feelers, doers, or some combination of the three, but we all have scads of room for growth. Recognizing the validity of the perspectives of other Christians not of our own stripe is a good first step in such progress.[11] Vern Poythress writes that it is this kind of multiperspectivalism that "offers a radical challenge for growth"[12] to the Reformed church and encourages us to "listen sympathetically to other perspectives."[13] Is this not the summons of the Reformation slogan *semper reformanda* ("always reforming")? And might this not be what it means for us to "have love for one another" (John 13:35) and "do good to everyone, and especially to those who are of the household of faith" (Gal. 6:10)? Poythress expands:

---

[9]John M. Frame, "Machen's Warrior Children," available at http://www.frame-poythress.org/frame_articles/2003Machen.htm. Frame explains his title: "From 1923 to the present, the movement begun by J. Gresham Machen and Westminster Theological Seminary has supplied the theological leadership for the conservative evangelical Reformed Christians in the United States. Under that leadership, conservative Calvinists made a strong stand against liberal theology. But having lost that theological battle in the Presbyterian Church, U.S.A., they turned inward to battle among themselves about issues less important—in some cases, far less important—than liberalism." Later Frame comments, "Once the Machenites found themselves in a 'true Presbyterian church' they were unable to moderate their martial impulses. Being in a church without liberals to fight, they turned on one another. . . . The almost exclusive focus on doctrinal issues in many Reformed circles is itself part of the problem. As Tim Keller advises, Reformed Christianity needs a vision that encompasses not only doctrinal statements, but also our piety, evangelistic outreach, and missions of mercy."
[10]Ibid.
[11]For Poythress's book-length treatment of this theme, see his *Symphonic Theology: The Validity of Multiple Perspectives in Theology* (Phillipsburg, NJ: P&R, 1987).
[12]Vern Poythress, "Multiperpectivalism and the Reformed Faith," in *Speaking the Truth in Love: The Theology of John M. Frame*, ed. John J. Hughes (Phillipsburg, NJ: P&R, 2009), 199.
[13]Ibid., 180.

If you love your neighbor, you are willing to listen to him sympathetically. And if you listen, you begin to understand his perspective. Maybe you find some erroneous thinking. But you also find some positive insights. When you find insights, you incorporate your neighbor's perspective into your own thinking, and then you have two perspectives instead of one. . . . Multiperspectivalism can be seen as little more than a self-conscious description and codification of some of the processes that are innate in loving your neighbor.[14]

Listening Sympathetically and Avoiding Infighting

When *Christianity Today* asked Billy Graham in January 2011 what he saw as the most important issues facing evangelicals today, he responded:

The most important issue we face today is the same the church has faced in every century: Will we reach our world for Christ? In other words, will we give priority to Christ's command to go into all the world and preach the gospel? Or will we turn increasingly inward, caught up in our own internal affairs or controversies, or simply becoming more and more comfortable with the status quo? Will we become inner-directed or outer-directed? The central issues of our time aren't economic or political or social, important as these are. The central issues of our time are moral and spiritual in nature, and our calling is to declare Christ's forgiveness and hope and transforming power to a world that does not know him or follow him. May we never forget this.[15]

Will the Western church heed the Great Commission call to disciple the nations, or will we "turn increasingly inward, caught up in our own internal affairs or controversies"? Might it be that, as our context continues to become increasingly post-Christian and progressively awakens our collective awareness to the global-spiritual battle lines with Islam, new atheism, viral secularism, and pervasive pragmatism, we realize that our differences on tertiary issues (and many considered secondary) with fellow lovers of Jesus's biblical person and work are not as towering as we once thought?

---

[14]Ibid., 181.
[15]Available at http://www.christianitytoday.com/ct/2011/januaryweb-only/qabillygraham.html?start=2.

The Challenge Ahead

With this book's editors being happily Reformed, our starting place, not surprisingly, is the life of the mind. But from that starting point, we hope to incorporate the heart and the hands and demonstrate the interconnectedness of our thinking, loving, and doing. Also, this volume began as a conference called "Think: The Life of the Mind and the Love of God" hosted by Desiring God in October 2010 based on, and celebrating the release of, John Piper's book by the same title.[16] The following chapters are revised and expanded forms of the plenary messages at that conference.[17]

In the pages that follow, Rick Warren, R. C. Sproul, Albert Mohler, Thabiti Anyabwile, Francis Chan, and John Piper challenge us to pursue holistic Christianity. They want us to be thinkers—very engaged and serious thinkers—and more. To be feelers, with great passion for Jesus and his gospel, and more. And doers, endeavoring great acts of love for others, and more. Our Savior perfectly embodies all three and demonstrates that thinking, feeling, and doing indeed are not at odds but mutually strengthening and reinforcing.

Thinking: Warren, Mohler, and Sproul

In the first three chapters, Warren, Mohler, and Sproul issue a pointed challenge for rigorous thinking. Warren's chapter, "The Battle for Your Mind," draws our attention to the spiritual realities at work in pursuing the mind of Christ. Satan will not soon admit defeat against his remarkably significant foe in the mind captured for Jesus. Warren gives us four principles for victory in this spiritual warfare and also points us to five levels of learning, as well as issues a memorable closing challenge to dream.

Mohler takes us to Romans 1 and helps our minds see the effects of sin everywhere—not only in others but also in the mirror, within our very own minds. Along the way, we get fourteen effects of the fall on our minds and close with twelve features of the natural mind. R. C. Sproul then addresses the role of biblical revelation in the

---

[16]John Piper, *Think: The Life of the Mind and the Love of God* (Wheaton, IL: Crossway, 2010).
[17]More information on the conference, as well as the audio and video from the sessions, is available at http://www.desiringgod.org/events/national-conferences/2010.

growth and life of the mind. He takes a surprising approach in this chapter, as he explains the background to Paul's sermon on Mars Hill. I hope you will find it as illuminating and helpful as I do.

Doing: Anyabwile and Chan

Next we move toward doing, with our footing still firmly in the life of the mind. Anyabwile, a former Muslim, addresses the massive (and increasingly relevant) global reality of Islam. He tackles the tough topic of good and bad pluralism and gives us a glimpse into the heart of Islam and why it is inconsistent with even good pluralism. He closes by leading us to a Christian response that proves intensely practical—including the important reminder to engage with the simple, spoken gospel—*the* power of God for Muslim salvation (Rom. 1:16).

Chan then rattles our cages with a highly testimonial exposition of 1 Corinthians 8:1–3. Given that a large portion of the readers of this book consider themselves thinkers—after all, reading and thinking go together, as we have seen—Chan's chapter may be the kind of slap in the face we need and appreciate. Here we self-proclaimed thinkers might find ourselves jarred awake by how the wrong use of knowledge turns us away from serving others. The flipside is that the right use of knowledge is taken into the service of acts of love.

Loving: Piper

Finally, Piper's concluding chapter moves us from the life of the mind to the passions of the heart under the title "Thinking for the Sake of Joy: The Life of the Mind and the Love of God." He ends our study with the most important place to focus our thinking and feeling, and the final power source for our Christian doing, namely, the cross of Christ. The death of Jesus for sinners is the fullest, richest, deepest, clearest revelation of God in history. Piper writes, "There is no other place [than the cross of Christ] where you can see him more clearly or love him more dearly. Here is the place where your thinking will be most deeply purified and the worth of God will be most fully magnified."

These contributors bring a wealth of perspective and experience in calling for readers to glorify God and love others with heart *and* mind *and* hands. We pray that the pages ahead would be a Spirit-aided means toward holistic sanctification in your journey toward becoming a better thinker, feeler, and doer—for the glory of God in Christ.

1

The Battle for Your Mind

RICK WARREN

A violent battle is raging around us twenty-four hours per day.

In 1965, Donald Grey Barnhouse wrote a book about it called *The Invisible War*. It is the battle for your mind, and that battle is vicious. It is intense. It is unrelenting, and it is unfair because Satan never plays fair. And the reason why it is so intense is that your greatest asset is your mind.

Destroying Strongholds

I have seen the face of mental illness. I have seen what it is like when people are unable to hear God because their minds are broken and cannot seem to connect to God even when they want to connect to God. And I know whatever gets your mind gets you. So one of the most important things we need to learn and teach others is how to guard, strengthen, and renew our minds, because the battle for sin always starts in the mind.

There are many passages in Scripture that we could look at in this chapter, but I want us to focus in on one, 2 Corinthians 10:3–5:

> Though we walk in the flesh, we are not waging war according to the flesh [in other words, we don't fight with armor, we don't fight with politics, we don't fight with money, we don't fight with all the humanistic ways]. For the weapons of our warfare are not of the flesh but have divine power to destroy strongholds. We destroy

arguments and every lofty opinion raised against the knowledge of God, and take every thought captive to obey Christ.

The apostle Paul says here that our job in this battle is to "destroy strongholds." You know what a stronghold is? It is a mental block. Paul is talking about pretentions, arguments set up against the knowledge of God. This is a mental battle. And he says, "Destroy these strongholds." A stronghold can be one of two things:

- It can be a worldview, such as materialism, hedonism, Darwinism, secularism, relativism, communism, atheism. All of the different -isms are mental strongholds that people set up against the knowledge of God.
- A stronghold can also be a personal attitude. Worry can be a stronghold. Seeking the approval of other people can be a stronghold. Anything that you make an idol in your life can be a stronghold—fear, guilt, resentment, insecurity. All of these things can be strongholds in your mind. And the Bible says that we are to tear them down.

Taking Every Thought Captive

Now look at the very last phrase in the passage: "take every thought captive to obey Christ." Take captive every thought. The Greek word *aichmalōtizō* there means "to control, to conquer, to bring into submission." We *take captive*. We make it submit. Every thought obedient to Christ. Make it *obedient*. *Hupakōe* means "to bring into submission, to bring under control."

But how do you do that? And how do you teach other people to do that? How do I make my mind mind? I have noticed that my mind doesn't always mind. It is often disobedient. It is often very rebellious. It wants to go in a different direction. When I want to think a certain way, it wants to go another way. When I need to ponder, it wants to wander. When I need to pray, my thoughts want to float away. Paul talks about this in Romans 7, and he says, "I do not do the good I want, but the evil I do not want is what I keep on doing. . . . Wretched man that I am!" (Rom. 7:19, 24). The fact is, the reason we have so many ineffective Christians today is that they do not know how to fight the battle of the mind. And I blame pastors like me for that. We must spend more time teaching our people how to fight the battle of the mind.

Four Principles for Winning the Battle for Your Mind

I have been studying this subject for thirty-three years. I did my first study on the mind in 1977, working through all the books of the Bible. I think I could teach on this subject for an entire week. There is so much material on what the Bible has to say about strengthening our minds, renewing our minds, submitting our minds, and bringing our thoughts into captivity. There are at least one hundred principles in God's Word that have to do with what we are to do with our minds. As I said, your mind is your greatest asset.

But all I want to do in this chapter is give you four simple principles—four of the many, many principles that I have tried to teach to others over the years—for living like Christ and being effective for him.

1) Don't Believe Everything You Think

We naturally feel that if we think something, it must be true because it comes from within us. But just because you think something does not make it true. As I said above, I have seen the face of mental illness. So many different suggestions can come into the mind. The world puts suggestions in our minds that are false, and we are bombarded with those false ideas all the time. And, of course, Satan makes suggestions all the time. But your problem is much deeper than Satan. Everybody has a mental illness. We are all mentally ill. The mental illness is called sin. And the Bible uses at least a dozen different phrases for the condition of our minds under sin. Our minds are:

- confused (Deut. 28:20)
- anxious, closed (Job 17:3–4)
- evil, restless (Eccles. 2:21–23)
- rash, deluded (Lev. 5:4; Isa. 32:4 NIV)

The Bible talks about:

- a troubled mind (2 Kings 6:11)
- a depraved mind (1 Tim. 6:5)
- a sinful mind (Rom. 8:7 NIV)
- a dull mind (2 Cor. 3:14 NIV)
- a blinded mind (2 Cor. 4:4)
- a corrupt mind (2 Tim. 3:8)

Our Broken Minds

Our minds are broken by sin. Which means we cannot trust even what we think, ourselves. Jeremiah 17:9 says, "The heart is deceitful above all things, and desperately sick; who can understand it?" We have an amazing ability to lie to ourselves. You do it all the time. So do I. We lie. We tell ourselves that things aren't as bad as they really are. We tell ourselves that things are better than they really are. We tell ourselves that we're doing okay when we're not doing okay. We're telling ourselves it's no big deal when it is a big deal. In fact, the Bible tells us that you cannot be trusted to tell yourself the truth. That's why you need to question your own thoughts and teach others not to believe everything they think.

Just because you get a thought doesn't mean it's correct. This is the reason why we have so many fallen Christian leaders, because all sin begins with a lie. The Bible says Satan is "the father of lies" (John 8:44). And if he can get you to believe a lie, he can get you to sin. Anytime you sin, you are thinking that you know better than God. God has said this, but what about that? And so you have to question what you think. First John 1:8 says, "If we say we have no sin, we deceive ourselves, and the truth is not in us." We deceive ourselves all the time.

TRUE, REAL, GENUINE

Preconditioned to Misunderstand

I have noticed how the next generation values authenticity. I would like to ask, when has inauthenticity ever been in style? Authenticity has always been an attractive quality. But a lot of those proudly promoting their authenticity don't realize what it really is. You are not authentic until you can publicly admit how inauthentic you are most of the time. Authenticity begins when you start by admitting that you are inauthentic.

We all have blind spots. Some of us have bald spots, but we all have blind spots. We can't always tell ourselves the truth, because we don't stop to really think. Frequently we make snap judgments. We fail to notice important details. We all have more background biases than we realize. We jump to conclusions, and the Bible talks about this in Romans 2. We get trapped by categories—*Are you this or that?*—when whoever said there are only two categories or only three categories? We miss the big picture.

But one of the big reasons why you need to not believe everything you think is that we see what we want to see. I read whatever I can about the brain, and one of the things I just learned is that the optic nerve, which is the only nerve that goes directly to your brain, actually sends more impulses from your brain forward than from your eye backward. Which means your brain is telling you what you see. You are already preconditioned. That is why you can put four people at an accident and each of them will see something different. We must remind ourselves, and teach others, not to believe everything we think!

2) Guard Your Mind from Garbage

The second thing to learn in this battle for the mind is guarding your mind from garbage. The old cliché from the early days of the computer—GIGO, garbage in/garbage out—is still true today. If you put bad data into a computer, you will get bad results out. If you put mental garbage into your mind, you will get garbage out in your life. Proverbs 15:14: "A wise person is hungry for knowledge, while the fool feeds on trash" (NLT). That might be a good verse to write on a Post-it note and stick on your television. And remember that the next time you think about going to a movie.

Any nutritionist will tell you that there are three kinds of food for your physical body. There is brain food that makes you smarter (food that actually makes you smarter!). There is junk food, which is simple calories—it's not poison, but it's just empty calories. And then there are toxic foods, which are poison.

The same is true in what you see, what you hear, and what you allow into your mind. Some food is brain food. It will make you smarter, more godly, and more mature emotionally. Then there is junk food. There is so much you can fill your mind with that really is just stuffing. It is neither good nor bad, as 1 Corinthians 6:12 says, lawful but not helpful. In other words, some things aren't necessarily wrong, but they aren't necessary. The Bible tells us to fill our minds with the right things. If you want to be healthy and "successful" in the Christian life and in ministering to others, successful in your ministry, fix your mind on the right things.

By the way, some people say, "God hasn't called me to be successful. He's called me to be faithful." That's just not true. The Bible says God expects not only faithfulness but also fruitfulness. Trace it through Scriptures. "I chose you . . . that you should go and bear fruit" (John 15:16). Jesus cursed a fig tree because it didn't bear fruit (Matt. 21:19)—that's how important fruitfulness is. Faithfulness is only half the equation. God expects fruitfulness as well.

Psalm 101:3 says, "I will not set before my eyes anything that is worthless." I know you would never invite a couple to come over to your house and ask them, "Why don't you commit an act of adultery right here in front of us?" But you do it every time you watch a TV program that has adultery in it. You would never invite somebody, "Why don't you murder somebody right here in my living room?" But you do it every time you watch a TV show in which somebody murders. How do you guard your mind against garbage? How do you help others guard their minds against garbage? Some people are so open-minded that their brains fall out. They think they can allow anything into their mind, and they will be just fine. They're kidding themselves.

Two Ways to Guard Our Minds

Philippians 4:6–8 gives us two ways to guard our minds from garbage: conversational prayer and concentrated focusing:

> Do not be anxious about anything, but in everything by prayer and supplication with thanksgiving let your requests be made known to God. And the peace of God, which surpasses all understanding, will guard your hearts and your minds in Christ Jesus. Finally, brothers, whatever is true, whatever is honorable, whatever is just, whatever is pure, whatever is lovely, whatever is commendable, if there is any excellence, if there is anything worthy of praise, think about these things.

How do you know when you have the peace that "surpasses all understanding"? When you give up trying to understand fully why God does what he does and simply trust him. This peace "will guard your hearts and your minds."

The first way you guard your heart and mind is "in everything" to pray. Then Paul says to think about "whatever is true, whatever is honorable, whatever is just, whatever is pure, whatever is lovely, whatever is commendable, if there is any excellence, if there is anything worthy of praise." Notice that he says to pray about everything. If you were to pray as much as you worry, you would have a lot less to worry about. *Don't worry about anything, but pray about everything.* This kind of prayer is like a running conversation—which means we are not on our knees. We don't close our eyes.

I have trained myself to do this. I talk to God all the time. I'm talking to him while I'm writing to you. You can develop a two-track mind. The average person can speak about 150 words per minute, but the average mind can understand about 350 words per minute—that is a 200-word per minute boredom factor. So you can certainly talk to God and talk to somebody else at the same time. So pray about everything. Maintain a running conversation.

Second, Paul says that we should fix our thoughts. "Think about these things." How do you do that? By concentrated focusing. This is one of the keys to overcoming temptation: don't merely resist it; replace it. Whatever you merely resist persists. The more you hit a nail, the harder you drive it into the wood. And when people say *I don't want to think about this*, what are they doing? They are thinking about it! And whatever gets your focus gets you. James tells us that "sin when it is fully grown brings forth death" (James 1:15). So don't merely resist it.

When I was a little kid, and I knew my mother had baked cookies, I would go up to the edge of the kitchen counter, and she would say, "Now, Ricky, don't eat those cookies." I would say, "I'm not, Mom. I'm just looking." I'm looking. I don't want it. I don't want it. And then I would grab it and eat it. Don't just resist; replace. Change the channel. Refocus. In the words of Thomas Chalmers, it is "the expulsive power of a new affection" that turns your mind away from the things that the Devil wants you to focus on to the things that God wants you to focus on. Guard your mind from garbage is the second key.

3) Never Let Up on Learning

The third thing to learn and teach to others in this battle for the mind is to never let up on learning. Become a lifelong learner. Love knowledge. Love wisdom. Learn to love the act of learning. The word *disciple* means "learner." You cannot be a disciple of Christ without being a learner. Jesus said, "Come to me, all who labor and are heavy laden [by the way, that sounds like a felt need!], and I will give you rest. Take my yoke upon you, and learn from me" (Matt. 11:28–29). What do you do when you take on a yoke? You share a burden with another animal. You lighten a load. And Jesus wants us to learn from him.

Many people act as though their education ended at their last graduation. I have met some pastors who have not cracked a book since seminary. They have never studied anything else. They have never taken another class since finishing school. Are you kidding me? To be a disciple means to be a learner. All leaders must first be disciples. So leaders must first be learners. The moment you stop learning, you stop leading. Growing churches require growing pastors. The moment you stop growing, your church stops growing.

You can learn from anybody if you just know the right questions. The Bible says, "Counsel in the heart of man is like deep water; but a man of understanding will draw it out" (Prov. 20:5 KJV). In other words, you can learn from anybody if you just learn to draw out his or her knowledge. And how do you do it? You draw it out by asking questions. We all know things that others don't, and others know things of which we are ignorant. That's why the Bible says, "Iron sharpens iron" (Prov. 27:17).

Humility Needed

But if you are going to really learn, you need one quality in particular: humility. Why does God resist the proud and give grace to the humble (1 Pet. 5:5)? Because the humble are teachable. I would rather admit that I don't know it all than to pretend that I know it all and not learn. You can learn from anybody. I learn from churches larger than Saddleback. I learn from churches smaller than Saddleback. I learn from guys older than me and from guys younger. I learn from people who don't like me. I learn from critics. I learn from people who totally misunderstand me. You can learn from anybody. Learning from your enemies is a way to be smarter than your enemies, because if your enemies learn only from themselves, but you learn from them, then you will know more than they do—what they know plus what you know!

Proverbs 18:15 (ICB) says, "The mind of a smart person is eager to get knowledge [that's a mark of intelligence!], and the wise person listens to learn more." We need to be eager to learn and willing to listen. Learn this old cliché: "God gave us two ears and one mouth," so we should listen twice as much as we speak. Proverbs 10:14 says, "Wise men store up knowledge" (NIV). In Scripture, knowledge is the only thing we are supposed to store up. Jesus says we are not to store up money. Don't store up treasure. Don't store up material possessions where moth and rust decay. But store up knowledge because knowledge is far more important than money. You can always get more money, but knowledge is something you are going to take with you to heaven. You will leave all your material wealth behind, but a wealth of knowledge goes with you.

Suggestions for Growing in Knowledge

One of the ways you can store up knowledge is to start a family library—a godly family library—and leave it as a legacy to the next generation. In my family, four generations back gave their library to three generations back, who gave it to two generations back—my dad—who gave it to me. I began collecting books when I was sixteen years old. For many years, I read a book a day. Today I have over twenty thousand volumes in my library. As a teenager I heard, "The impact on your life will be largely from the people you meet and the books you read." So I decided to get very intentional about both of those—whom I would meet and what I would read. And when you begin to build a library of godly, Christian books, you are leaving a legacy for the next generation. Twice in the book of Proverbs we are told to "store up my commands within you" (Prov. 2:1; 7:1 NIV). If you are going into eternity, you are going to take that with you.

If you're serious about growing in knowledge and growing in your mind, here's the approach I suggest:

- Read 25 percent of your books from the first fifteen hundred years of church history. So many people act like nothing happened between the times of Paul and Luther. God was at work all that time, and we are dismissing the God of the church to think that he was not having his Word faithfully taught during those times.
- Read 25 percent from the last five hundred years, since the Reformation.
- Read 25 percent from the last one hundred years.
- Read only 25 percent from contemporary authors of the last ten years.

A lot of people know all the contemporary books and none of the classics. Jesus did not just begin building his church in the year 2000. He has been working in and through his body for two millennia, and you can save yourself a lot of time if you will avail yourself of the whole tradition. It is wise to learn from experience, but it is wiser to learn from the experiences of others. It is also easier! It saves a lot of time and saves us from making the mistakes of others.

Read, Read, Read

I'm constantly reading. Every year I read through the complete works of a great thinker. In 2009 I read through twenty-six volumes of Jonathan Edwards. In 2010 I read through *Church Dogmatics*, the complete works of Karl Barth. I've read through John Wesley and through several other leaders. It is prideful to think that leaders from the past don't have anything to teach us. There really is nothing new under the sun. If it's held forth as new, then it's not true, because truth is eternal. It was true a thousand years ago. It will be true a thousand years from now.

Truth is never invented; it is only discovered. And if God has shown it as truth, somebody else in the church has seen it before. In fact, if you ever come up with a truth that nobody else has ever seen, I can tell you this: you're wrong.

The Bible says "Wise men store up knowledge" (Prov. 10:14 NIV). And here's Proverbs 19:8: "Whoever gets sense loves his own soul; he who keeps understanding will discover good." We must make time to think. Plan it in your life. Strategize for a balance between doing and thinking. We need both of them in our lives.

Five Levels of Learning

Let me overview quickly what I call "the five levels of learning." This is the pedagogy of discipleship that I have used for thirty years. It's a major reason why our church has been able to bring so many people in the front door and send so many out the back door on ministry and mission. I believe you can judge the health of a church not by its seating capacity but by its sending capacity. You don't judge the health of an army by how many soldiers sit in the mess hall and eat every week and listen to your Bible study. You judge the health of an army by how many are on frontlines doing battle in the world. We want to be able to bring them in, build them up, train them forward, and send them out. And to do so, we must be able to teach people not only to love the Word but also to do the Word (James 1:22–25). Here are what I call "the five levels of learning":

1) Knowledge
2) Perspective (Wisdom)
3) Conviction
4) Character
5) Skill

The first two have to do with knowing. The second two have to do with being. And the third one has to do with doing. You can use these as a template for all of your discipleship—moving people from "come and see" to "come and die."

1) KNOWLEDGE

First, we need to learn *knowledge*. God says in Hosea 4:6, "My people are destroyed for lack of knowledge." When we don't know the Word of God, we can be destroyed. And we need to know not only the Bible but also church history. That's why our church features each week on the back of the bulletin a figure from history, just a little bio. Also, we have a theological word of the week on the back of our bulletin because we want the people to know theological words and the great saints of church history. That's part of *knowledge*.

Sadly, you can learn the Bible without really knowing it; in other words, you can know all the facts without really knowing the content. You don't really know something until you apply it. That's why Jesus implies to the Pharisees that their problem isn't that they don't know Scripture but that they don't know the power of God (Mark 12:24). Think about what a rebuke that was to the Pharisees who had memorized the Pentateuch—Genesis, Exodus, Leviticus, Numbers, Deuteronomy. They had memorized it, yet Jesus says that their problem is that they don't know the Scripture. They needed to teach others their knowledge, teach others to love knowledge, and get rid of anti-intellectualism. (By the way, we need great Christian intellectuals today more than ever before—people a lot brighter than I!—who battle on the intellectual level against the many competing worldviews.)

2) PERSPECTIVE (WISDOM)

The second thing we need is perspective. The Bible calls this perspective "wisdom." Wisdom is found in seeing life from God's viewpoint. It is seeing from God's perspective. Knowledge is knowing what God does; wisdom and perspective are knowing why he does it. Knowledge is the bottom rung; perspective is the next building block above it.

Some churches are great at Bible knowledge but fail to teach their people perspective. They don't teach wisdom. I love this paraphrase of Isaiah 55:8 in *The Message*: God says, "I don't think the way you think. The way you work isn't the way I work." Obviously that's true! Psalm 103:7 says that the Lord "made known his ways unto Moses, his acts unto the children of Israel" (KJV). God revealed his acts. The children of Israel saw the miracles. They saw the Red Sea split. They saw the water at Marah. They saw the doves and the manna and much more. They saw the acts of God. But Moses knew the ways of God. He knew why God had done those things. They had knowledge, but Moses also had perspective. In knowledge, the goal is to know the Word of God; but in perspective, the goal is to have the mind of God as much as possible. So we want to develop for ourselves, and to help others develop, the mind of Christ (1 Cor. 2:14–16; Phil. 2:5–11).

3) CONVICTION

The third thing we need is conviction. Conviction is the third building block, as these build on each other. We pursue knowledge of the Word, then perspective on why God does what he does, and, in doing so, we start to develop convictions.

What is God's perspective on temptation? What is God's perspective on evil? What is God's perspective on our past, our present, and our future? What is God's perspective on sin? What is God's perspective on Satan? Once we start getting perspective, we begin developing convictions.

Conviction is not opinion. Opinion is something you argue about; conviction is something you die for. And what we need today as much as ever are men and women of godly, biblical convictions. If you know hardly anything about history, you can still know that the people who have had the greatest impact on our world for good or evil were not the smartest, not those who had the most knowledge, not the wealthiest, not the most talented, but those who have had the deepest convictions for right or wrong. And, of course, it is Jesus who has made the most impact, and it is Jesus who had the deepest convictions of all.

If you want to know how much Jesus loves you, look at the cross.

With arms outstretched and nail-pierced hands, Jesus says that the cross is how much he and his Father love us. "God shows his love for us in that while we were still sinners, Christ died for us" (Rom. 5:8). "I love you so much it hurts," he says. "I love you so much that every drop of blood falling to the ground says, 'I love you.'" That's conviction.

Paul talks in 1 Corinthians 7 about being settled in our own minds, which means having godly convictions. And in Hebrews 11:1, faith is said to be "the conviction of things not seen." Let me give you some examples.

- "[Nothing] . . . will be able to separate us from the love of God" (Rom. 8:39). That's conviction. It's not an opinion; it's a conviction.
- "And we know that for those who love God all things work together for good, for those who are called according to his purpose. For those whom he foreknew he also predestined to be conformed to the image of his Son, in order that he might be the firstborn among many brothers" (Rom. 8:28–29). That's a conviction, not an opinion.
- "It is more blessed to give than to receive" (Acts 20:35). That's a conviction.
- "I know whom I have believed, and am persuaded that he is able to keep that which I have committed unto him against that day" (2 Tim. 1:12 KJV). That's a conviction. We need men and women of conviction.
- And there is this great conviction: "Though he slay me, yet will I trust in him" (Job 13:15 KJV). *I don't have to understand it*, Job says, *but I'm going to trust God no matter what.*

In conviction we want the heart of God. We don't want only to see what God sees but also to feel what God feels—about the world, about the lost, about his Word, about his church. We need to learn knowledge. Then we need to add to that God's perspective. But then we need to add to the convictions that come out of knowing the mind of God.

4) CHARACTER

Once we begin to develop convictions, we start developing habits—and the sum total of our habits is what we can call "character." We cannot say that we have the character of honesty unless we are habitually honest. We cannot say we have the character of kindness unless we are habitually kind. Character is the sum total of our habits.

If I were to say to my wife, "Honey, I'll be faithful to you twenty-nine days of the month," she knows, and I know, that partial faithfulness is unfaithfulness. It is only faithfulness if it is my habit to always be faithful to her.

You develop character by developing the habits of love and joy and peace and patience—those nine qualities from Galatians 5—kindness, goodness, gentleness, faithfulness, and self-control (vv. 22–23). What are these fruit of the Spirit? They are a perfect picture of the character of Christ. If we want to become like Jesus, then we must seek the fruit of the Spirit in our lives. The goal is to become more like God in our character, not to become gods. We never will become God—no matter how much fruit we produce. We will never be mini-gods. We are not God. That's the oldest lie in the book, that we "will be like God" (Gen. 3:5). We need to learn character.

5) SKILL

When we begin to develop character and do good habitually—daily Bible reading, regular fasting, regular prayer, regular days of prayer, regular witnessing—when these become the habits of our lives, the more we do them, the better we will get at them. And so we come to the last level of learning: skill.

Skill comes through doing something over and over and over. Ecclesiastes 10:10 says, "If the ax is dull and its edge unsharpened, more strength is needed, but skill will bring success" (NIV). That is one of my "life verses." If you are chopping wood, it helps to have a sharp ax. If you have a dull ax, it takes more energy to cut the wood. But if you have a sharp ax, it doesn't take as much energy. "Skill will bring success." It doesn't say here that prayer will bring success. It doesn't say that desire will bring success. It doesn't say it's dedication. But *skill* will bring success. A farmer can pray all he wants, but if he tries to harvest a wheat field with a grape picker, the job will not get done. We must have the right skills.

I know many men who are godly and love Jesus and preach

the Bible, but their churches are dying on the vine. The Bible says skill will bring success. We are never wasting our time when we are sharpening our ax. That's why I challenge you to go to conferences and learn from anybody and everybody. We don't only need to know the Word of God, but we also want to have the mind of God and the heart of God and to develop the character of God—and we want to do the will of God. "Be doers of the word, and not hearers only" (James 1:22).

I have said it before, and I'll write it here again: we need another Reformation—and this one needs to be about *deeds*, not creeds. Many have misunderstood me and said, "Oh, he doesn't believe in creeds!" I believe in creeds. I preach on creeds with frequency. But the issue is not creeds alone. *Creeds must be turned into deeds*. It's not one or the other. It's both. We must do and teach the kind of behavior that goes with sound doctrine. We must be doers of the Word.

We only believe the parts of the Bible that we actually *do*. You may say, "I believe in witnessing." Do you do it? No? Then you don't really believe in it. "I believe in tithing." Do you do it? No? Then you don't really believe in it. "I believe in having family devotions." Do you do it? No? Then you don't really believe in it. *We only believe what we actually do*. And our problem is that we know far more than we do and we teach people too much. Mark this. We might be teaching people so much that they aren't able to apply it.

I grew up in the Southern Baptist Church. First thing Sunday morning I would go to Sunday school, and there I was supposed to get an application that changed my life. Then I would go to morning service, and I'd get another application that was supposed to change my life. Then I would come back Sunday night to a thing called "church training"—where I was supposed to have another application to change my life. And then in the evening service was another application to change my life. That's four in one day! Then I was supposed to come back to midweek prayer and Bible study and get another application. Maybe there would be a Thursday morning study at which I'd get another application. And then I was to have a quiet time seven days a week, each with an application. That's about fourteen applications a week.

Friend, our lives do not change that much that fast. I am doing well if I get one good application a week. The problem in many of our churches is that before we genuinely apply last week's message, or this morning's message, we are already coming back and learning (or teaching) something else. We are taking notes and filling notebooks and thinking that because we are writing things down, we are really getting it. But we're not. A wide gap exists between knowing and doing in American Christianity—and perhaps its cause is too much teaching. Before we actually apply what we have learned, we are on to the next thing, and we cannot handle it. We cannot change that much that fast.

Another weakness of the church today when it comes to learning is that often we pastors are not teaching our people to be self-feeders. We do all the feeding instead of teaching the sheep how to feed themselves. We each need to learn for ourselves the skills of doing a systematic Bible study, a thematic study, and a book synthesis. How do you analyze a chapter? What are the steps in doing a word study? What are the steps in how to do a biographical study? We preachers can do a lot of ought-to preaching without giving our people the how-to's.

While I was growing up, my dad was on the staff of a seminary. So I heard more sermons growing up than most people. And as I heard all these sermons, I would write over and over again as I was taking notes, "*YBH, YBH, YBH*"—yes, but how? Interpretation without application is abortion. We may be teaching people to have big heads and little hands and little hearts and little feet. We must apply the Word of God. Jesus gave the how-tos; he taught people how to do it. Isaiah 26:3 says, "You keep him in perfect peace whose mind is stayed on you, because he trusts in you." Your mental state depends on what you think about. Keep your mind fixed on the Word of God, the mind of God, the convictions of God, the character of God, and the skills of God.

4) Let God Stretch Your Imagination

One final area I would like to address before closing this chapter is the imagination. If we are going to learn, and teach others, how to fight the battle for the mind, we must learn how to let God stretch our imaginations. This is a part of the battle. This is part of thinking. Everything that happens in life begins with a dream. Somebody has to imagine it first. This is a gift that God gave to us: the ability to dream and envision and imagine something before it comes into reality. Every building we see was first imagined by an architect before it was built. Every piece of art was imagined before it was painted. Every song was imagined before it was written. Every athletic award, every gold medal, the athlete imagined before it ever happened. Every church that's been started, somebody—either a group of people or a single church planter—imagined that church first. Rarely does anything happen until somebody starts dreaming.

We need to become great, godly dreamers. Proverbs 29:18 says, "Where there is no prophetic vision the people cast off restraint." The word "vision" relates to dreaming. It means a kind of revelation, a vision from God. And where there's not this vision, this God-directed dreaming, the people "cast off restraint"—literally, they get "out of control." When we do not have an overarching vision or dream or goal for our lives, our lives are out of control. What we need today are great dreamers.

My prayer is that Acts 2:17 will be true in your life and in your church: "And in the last days it shall be, God declares, that I will pour out my Spirit on all flesh, and your sons and your daughters shall prophesy, and your young men shall see visions, and your old men shall dream dreams." Let me ask you quite frankly: What's your dream for your next ten years? Have you even written it down? Thoughts get disentangled when they go through the lips and the fingertips. If you haven't written it down, you haven't really thought about it. Writing makes a man more precise. What is your dream for your family? What is your dream for you personally? How are you going to be different ten years from now?

Our church recently entered into what we're calling the "Decade of Destiny." We have written out our dreams for the character changes we want to see in our lives over the next ten years. What would you attempt for God if you knew you couldn't fail? What we need today are great imaginers. Each generation needs its C. S. Lewises and J. R. R.

Tolkiens, and G. K. Chestertons, and Tolstoys, and Dostoyevskys. We need great dreamers, great *imagineering* people. Be that where you are. We need these in science. We need the Boyles. We need the Pascals. We need the Maxwells in physics and the Keplers and the Calvins. We need it in business. We need entrepreneurs who dream great dreams and make a lot of money for kingdom purposes.

When I talk about dreaming great dreams, I am not talking about changing doctrine. The Bible says in Jude 3 that the biblical faith was "once for all delivered to the saints." The gospel is there, and we don't change it. To do so is heresy. But for those of us who are leaders, whether in the church or simply in our homes, what we don't see with our physical eyes is far more important than what we do see. I can attest to that after nearly forty years of leading. We can only do the impossible if we see the invisible.

You may have heard people say that what the mind can conceive, the hand can achieve. That's not fully true. There's a kernel of truth in it. But Einstein said that imagination is more important than knowledge. For what you imagine has no limit. Logic will get you from A to B, but imagination will take you everywhere. Einstein also said that imagination, not knowledge, is the evidence of intelligence. And Napoleon said that imagination rules the world. What we need today are people creating new innovations in a new society to reach new generations. The message must never change, but the methods have to change with every generation.

Innovation

Where does innovation come from? It comes from simply asking the right questions. The only difference between an innovator and anybody else is not that the innovator sees more than what everybody else sees but that he asks questions that nobody else does. Perhaps the biggest limitation on your growth and your ministry to others is your imagination. God cannot fulfill your dream if you don't have one. God cannot bless your vision if you don't have his vision for your life. God cannot help you reach a goal if you don't have a goal. A goal is a kind of statement of faith. "Without faith it is impossible to please" God (Heb. 11:6), and "whatever does not proceed from faith is sin"

(Rom. 14:23). The Bible says that "according to your faith be it done to you" (Matt. 9:29). And when we set goals, we are saying, *God, I believe you want me to accomplish this with your help by this time.* I am challenging you. I am daring you. I am begging you: dream great dreams for God, and teach others to dream great dreams for God.

It's not enough just not to believe everything we think. It's not enough just to guard our minds from the garbage. It's not enough to keep on learning and developing character. We must also let God develop our imagination. Because we must outthink and out-dream and outsmart the world for the glory of God—not for our private good but for the glory of God and the good of others. Paul says in Ephesians 3:20, "Now to him who is able to do far more abundantly than all that we ask or think"—more than we can imagine. More than we can dream. Infinitely beyond our highest prayers, desires, thoughts, or hopes. I think I'm a pretty big dreamer, but God says, "Think of the biggest thing you can think of, and I can top that. I can outdo that."

A Challenge to Thinkers and to Doers

Many of you are natural thinkers and love the world of thoughts and ideas. You may not really like people, but you love the world of thoughts and ideas. Maybe your idea of growth and of ministry is to stay in a study all week. For some pastors, this would mean going through a vacuum tube out to the pulpit, then preaching, and then taking the vacuum tube back to their study. That would be heaven for them.

Perhaps you are naturally a great thinker—God wired you that way. And then others of you are naturally great doers. You're figuring out how to do it—winning people to Christ, baptizing them in large numbers, planting churches, equipping servant leaders, assisting the poor, caring for the sick, educating the next generation, going out into the hurts and highways and byways of life and taking up the cross where people least expect it. You're a doer.

Here's what I want to say to you, friend. Those of you who are thinkers, you need to do more. Those of you who are doers, you need to think more. It's not one or the other. It's both-and.

THINK!

Let me leave you with this little acrostic: THINK. Here are five things to remember in our own lives and to teach to others.

"T" stands for *test every thought*. Psalm 139:23–24 says, "Search me, O God, and know my heart! Try me and know my thoughts! And see if there be any grievous way in me, and lead me in the way everlasting!" Ask God to search and test your thoughts. Don't believe everything you think. Test every thought.

"H" stands for *helmet your head*. Put on the helmet of salvation. In California you can't ride a motorcycle without wearing a helmet. You don't have to wear elbow pads or knee pads, but you do have to wear a helmet. Why? Because if you get your head hurt, you are in deep kimchi. And the Bible says, "Take the helmet of salvation" (Eph. 6:17). Until we are saved, we don't have any protection against the fiery darts that the Devil unleashes on our minds. Repentance means changing your mind—not just changing what you do. It's first and at its heart mind change. Repentance is changing the way you think. It is a mental shift. Put on the helmet of salvation.

"I" stands for *imagine great thoughts*. Think about all the great promises of God. Everything is possible to him who believes. What an amazing blank check we have in Christ. Imagine great thoughts.

"N" stands for *nourish a godly mind*. Make sure that you are growing and developing. Psalm 119:15 says, "I will meditate on your precepts and fix my eyes on your ways." Mediate and fix. Study and reflect.

"K" stands for *keep on learning*. The Bible says, "Practice these things, immerse yourself in them, so that all may see your progress" (1 Tim. 4:15). Do others see progress in your life? Are your words and conversations more powerful, more meaty, deeper, stronger, more practical, more life-touching?[1]

The Christian life is not just knowing; it's *being and doing*.

---

[1]Pastors reading this chapter may want to ask questions like the following of their sermons: (1) What is the knowledge of God and the knowledge of his Word that the people are learning in this sermon? (2) What is the perspective I'm teaching them in this sermon? (3) What are the convictions I want to get across? (4) What are the character qualities I want to develop? (5) What are the skills?

*   *   *

Heavenly Father,
Thank you for those who have read and engaged this chapter. I pray
that you would raise up a new generation of godly intellectuals who
know your Word, understand your mind, feel your heart, live out your
character, and do your will with skill.

Give us a new generation of imagineers. *Give us new imaginations in
science and in business and in missions and in architecture. And may
Christians be known for outthinking, outsmarting, and out-loving the
rest of the world.*

I pray a blessing on every man and woman reading these words.
Bless their families. Bless their churches. Bless their ministries.
Protect them from the Evil One. And as the battle for sin is fought
in their minds, may they not merely resist but refocus. May they fill
their minds with the washing of the water of the Word. May they be
transformed by the renewing of their minds so that they may know
your will—which is good and pleasing and perfect.

In Jesus's name I pray.
Amen

2

The Way the World Thinks:

Meeting the Natural Mind in the Mirror and in the Marketplace

R. ALBERT MOHLER JR.

In his book *Evangelicalism in Modern Britain: A History from the 1730s to the 1980s*, British historian David Bebbington provided a definition of evangelicalism that has become the standard boilerplate understanding for academics and journalists on both sides of the Atlantic.[1] He described evangelicalism in terms of four distinctives: biblicism (a confidence that the Bible is the Word of God), conversionism (a belief that persons must come to a saving knowledge of the Lord Jesus Christ), crucicentrism (a belief that the cross and the resurrection are the central acts whereby God saves sinners), and activism (evangelicals are people who hold crusades, build colleges and seminaries, go on mission trips, organize conferences, and create periodicals and publishing houses).

Noticeably absent from Bebbington's list, however, is the idea that evangelicals are defined by their thinking. This is to our shame. Christ's people are to be active in the "renewing of [the] mind," for "as [a man] thinketh in his heart, so is he" (Rom. 12:1–2 KJV; Prov. 23:7 KJV; Matt. 15:10–20). There is a necessary distinction between thinking and action, but if activism happens without an adequate

---

[1]David Bebbington, *Evangelicalism in Modern Britain: A History from the 1730s to the 1980s* (New York: Routledge, 1989), 2–3.

foundation of thinking, then our activism will be separated from the gospel and from the demands of Christ on our lives. Therefore, without apology, Christians must think about thinking.

Children do not often think about thinking. Within the developmental stage of early adolescence, there comes a sudden acknowledgment that there are other minds. "People think differently than I, or even my parents, think," a young teen will exclaim. By adolescence, we perceive ourselves thinking and begin to think about that process. Most human beings, however, never attempt to think deeply about thinking.

By contrast, a Christian understands that he or she was made to bring God glory, to point persons to Christ, to exalt in the things of Christ, and to meditate upon God's Word. Because of the biblical imperative to be transformed by the renewing of our minds, Christians must perpetually think about thinking. Philosophers call this a "second-order discipline." Thinking is a first-order discipline, but thinking about thinking is a second-order discipline. This complex thinking is required if we are to measure and contrast faithful thinking over against unfaithful thinking.

The Regenerate Mind and the Unregenerate Mind

One of the first steps in thinking about thinking is the realization that we *could* think in ways different than we do. This is the recognition that there are other peoples, worldviews, philosophies of life, and belief systems at work in the world. An essential part of our Christian faithfulness is the recognition of difference. Christians must also recognize the crucial distinction between the regenerate mind and the unregenerate mind. Those who have come to know salvation through Jesus Christ, who by God's grace have been united with Christ and seek to be faithful to the gospel, understand the difference between the before and after. Part of one's maturing in Christ is an intellectual growth away from former ways and patterns of thinking. There are beliefs, principles of thought, and axioms that must be left behind in order to be faithful to Christ.

Our faithfulness, however, is only part of the equation. We also seek to understand the mind of the age and the way that persons around us in the world are thinking, because we desperately want to communicate the gospel to them. Much like entering into a foreign culture, entering into our own culture requires us to step back and think carefully about how people think, discerning the operational rules, principles, and worldviews of the prevailing thought systems around us.

We face an intellectual crisis in the Western world. Given the pace of change in our age, anyone with the slightest intellectual perception can detect significant shifts in the worldview around us. An important conversation is being had about pre-modern, modern, and postmodern ways of thinking. We are facing a knowledge emergency, as people all around us are uncertain that it is possible to know anything. Many people hear the claim to knowledge as a political statement, while others seem unable to make any kind of differentiation between fact (knowledge) and value (preference). This knowledge emergency can be traced all the way back to the Enlightenment, when there was a giant shift in the way human beings thought. Although the shift did not immediately affect the cobblers of the time as much as it did the clergy and the academics, before too long the cobbler and the cobbler's children were also affected by forms of thought passed down from the educated elites of society.

We have now been in a postmodern crisis for a generation. Though the word is overused, postmodernism is itself rather inescapable. Just as there was a shift from pre-modern ways of thinking into modernity and the autonomous reign of reason, aspects of modernity have now shifted into something else. Therefore, above all, Christians need biblical grounding.

Thinking about Thinking (Romans 1:18–32)

Although there are many excellent and fitting texts of Scripture to guide us at this point, an examination of Romans 1:18–32 will serve us in our thinking about the epistemological crisis—the crisis of thinking and knowing. The apostle Paul writes:

> For the wrath of God is revealed from heaven against all ungodliness and unrighteousness of men, who by their unrighteousness

suppress the truth. For what can be known about God is plain to them, because God has shown it to them. For his invisible attributes, namely, his eternal power and divine nature, have been clearly perceived, ever since the creation of the world, in the things that have been made. So they are without excuse. For although they knew God, they did not honor him as God or give thanks to him, but they became futile in their thinking, and their foolish hearts were darkened. Claiming to be wise, they became fools, and exchanged the glory of the immortal God for images resembling mortal man and birds and animals and creeping things.

Therefore God gave them up in the lusts of their hearts to impurity, to the dishonoring of their bodies among themselves, because they exchanged the truth about God for a lie and worshiped and served the creature rather than the Creator, who is blessed forever! Amen.

For this reason God gave them up to dishonorable passions. For their women exchanged natural relations for those that are contrary to nature; and the men likewise gave up natural relations with women and were consumed with passion for one another, men committing shameless acts with men and receiving in themselves the due penalty for their error.

And since they did not see fit to acknowledge God, God gave them up to a debased mind to do what ought not to be done. They were filled with all manner of unrighteousness, evil, covetousness, malice. They are full of envy, murder, strife, deceit, maliciousness. They are gossips, slanderers, haters of God, insolent, haughty, boastful, inventors of evil, disobedient to parents, foolish, faithless, heartless, ruthless. Though they know God's decree that those who practice such things deserve to die, they not only do them but give approval to those who practice them.

In the context of this opening chapter of the book of Romans, the apostle Paul informs not only a first-century Roman congregation of Christians, but he also, by the inspiration of the Holy Spirit, teaches Christians throughout all the ages. Paul's story of universal human sinfulness and depravity is our story. In these words, we discover the explanation of how it is that we find ourselves in this condition of sinfulness. Furthermore, Paul explains that the great epistemological crisis is not as new and recent as we might think in our modern conceit; the knowledge crisis is ancient.

Paul speaks of the crisis as emerging and residing in the mind, but he also speaks as one armed with a confidence in the gospel of Jesus Christ. He writes, "For the wrath of God is revealed from heaven against all ungodliness and unrighteousness of men, who by their unrighteousness suppress the truth" (v. 18). This is information we desperately need to know. Paul tells us that sinful humanity is involved in a conspiracy, not of the few but of the many. Every single human being is part of the intellectual activity described here. All descendants of Adam are involved in the suppression of "truth in unrighteousness."

We do not like to think of ourselves as suppressors of truth, however. This is conveyed by the very name we have given ourselves: *Homo sapiens*, meaning "the wise thinking creature." Humans rightly view ourselves as set apart from the rest of creation because of intellectual capacity, but we also see ourselves as fair-minded people who think rightly. We tend to associate with people who think as we do because nothing reinforces the way we think as being with people who think like us.

The apostle Paul argues that the intellectual bent and ambition of human beings operate as mechanisms to suppress the truth. Granted, some people believe their great ambition is to find the truth. The Latin word for truth, *veritas*, is even placed on the seal of our great universities. Yet, despite our living in an age in which massive universities, educational upward mobility, post-Enlightenment science, and modern approaches to liberal arts masquerade as parts of a great quest for truth, Paul claims that humans do not merely suppress the truth; mankind suppresses the truth in *unrighteousness*. We do not suppress the truth simply because we do not want to deal with it. Instead, we work out the truth suppression conspiracy in a great cloud of unrighteousness.

Despite all of the rationalization, theorizing, and self-justification that derive from truth suppression, human beings remain accountable. Paul states, "For what can be known about God is plain to them, because God has shown it to them" (v. 19). The real knowledge crisis is not merely what people *do not* know; it is also what they *will not* know. It is a disposition of the will. Some modern schools of philosophy are even now catching onto this truth that the Bible had already made clear—the will is the great engine of the intellect. The conceit of the modern age was the belief that the intellect is neutral because human beings were viewed as basically good or morally neutral. That worldview saw ignorance as the great enemy and enlightenment as the answer. Enlightenment cannot be the answer, however, because the will drives the intellect.

Paul unfolds what theologians call natural, or general, revelation. He points to the fact that "what can be known about God is plain to them, because God has shown it to them" (v. 19). How is this so? "For his invisible attributes, namely, his eternal power and divine nature, have been clearly perceived, ever since the creation of the world, in the things that have been made. So they are without excuse" (v. 20). The knowledge of God is embedded in creation. Even his invisible attributes are made visible in creation. No one will be able to say, "I did not know." No one will have an excuse.

It is not just in the outer world of nature that the knowledge of God is apprehended, however. It is also in the inner world of the conscience. In the second chapter of Romans, Paul will deal with the reality of the conscience. The problem with our consciences is not that they are there; we should be thankful for that. Instead, the problem is that our will does not allow the conscience to operate as it was intended. We can make our conscience do what we want our conscience to do.

Undergirding all of this is an understanding of the *imago Dei*, knowing what it means to be made in the image of God. Our ability to know of God through general revelation is reflective of the *imago Dei*. The fact that we have a conscience is also reflective of the fact that we are made in the image of God. Indeed, we are set apart from creation and distinct from the other creatures.

As a boy, I loved to watch the television program *Mutual of Omaha's Wild Kingdom*, which would show the most bizarre and wonderful animals in their native habitat. As young boys are prone to do, the animals I loved to see were the lions and tigers. After a few shots of the predator, an unsuspecting flock of antelope would be shown. The lion, hidden in the grass, would then leap out with unbelievable energy upon one of the antelope, overtake it, and kill it. But in thinking back over the many depictions of carnivore meals I saw, I do not recall ever seeing one of those lions step back from the carcass and say, "Wow, I do not know what is in me sometimes. That was so violent. There has to be some way of meeting my needs other than this. I need therapy." No, he just eats. There is no conscience whatsoever.

Nobody ever walks into his house only to be met by the family dog vehemently apologizing. A parent, however, knows that when the two-year-old cannot be found and is hiding behind the recliner, he is not playing hide-and-seek. The child, though young, knows that he has done something wrong. Humans make the conscience do what they want it to do. Unlike the animals, we are able to rationalize.

Continuing on, Paul states, "For although they knew God, they did not honor him as God or give thanks to him, but they became futile in their thinking, and their foolish hearts were darkened. Claiming to be wise, they became fools" (vv. 21–22). The effects of sin result in futility in thinking. Sinners who suppress the truth and ignore the revelation of God are characterized in their thinking by emptiness, vacuity, self-delusion, and rationalization—intellectual emptiness.

Monuments to human wisdom surround us. In the bookstore, one will find monuments to human wisdom. In the university, one will see the triumphs of human wisdom as a prominent theme. All this, of course, leads to idolatry—we have "exchanged the glory of the immortal God for images resembling mortal man and birds and animals and creeping things" (v. 23).

The sinful decline does not end there, however. Three times in verses 24–32, Paul uses the formula "God gave them up." He writes, "God gave them up in the lusts of their hearts to impurity" (v. 24). Then, "God gave them up to dishonorable passions" (v. 26) and then again "God gave them up to a debased mind to do what ought not to be done" (v. 28).

We often hear this passage taught as a warning to Rome, and other empires, that God is giving them over to their own sinfulness. Then, the application is brought to bear on the United States of

America, that if we follow in the pattern of Rome's sinful descent, God will likewise give us over in the same manner. This passage, however, is not about empires—Roman or American. This text is about humanity. The verb tense in the phrase "God gave" is past tense—this has *already* happened. God has given humanity over. The apostle Paul includes everyone in the indictment as he describes the giving over of all of humanity to sinfulness.

The Noetic Effects of the Fall

In the third chapter of Genesis, we read of the fall—the universal story that explains the intellectual crisis in which we find ourselves. In Adam's fall, we all fell. Adam and Eve demanded to know what they were not to know, and once they knew it, they knew themselves as rebels. They became the enemies of God. We do not rightly know who we are without the biblical revelation of the fall.

The consequences of the fall were enormous and immediate. First, the consequence of death created separation and alienation from God, and it resulted in eternal punishment. These cosmic consequences are made clear in the totality of Scripture. Then, there is the story of humanity's decline into total sinfulness and depravity, made clear even in the early chapters of the book of Genesis. The story moves quickly from the fall in Genesis 3 to the stories of Cain murdering Abel, the flood, the Tower of Babel, and others.

The great epistemological crisis goes back to the fall. The consequences of the fall on our thinking have been nothing less than devastating. Unfortunately, this is not readily apparent to us. We are now so distanced from accurate knowledge of ourselves that we do not even know how warped our thinking is.

Theologically, this is referred to as the noetic consequences of the fall. The phrase "noetic effects" refers to the intellectual consequences of sin. John Calvin said there were three great causes of this noetic disaster.[2] The first was the fall itself and its direct results. Adam and Eve had an intellectual crisis the very moment they sinned. The book of Genesis is very clear and candid in pointing us to their shame and

---

[2]Stephen K. Moroney, *The Noetic Effects of Sin: A Historical and Contemporary Exploration of How Sin Affects Our Thinking* (Lanham: Lexington, 1999).

to their knowledge—fig leaves and all. Second, Calvin pointed out that the church must always be aware that Satan wishes to confuse our thinking. We have an intellectual enemy whom we ignore at our peril. Third, we must recognize that God, for the protection of his own character, judges our minds in such a way that he gives us over to ignorance and falsehood. This is seen most crucially and centrally in idolatry.

What are the effects of sin and the fall upon our intellect? First, our reason is now opposed to God. This is one of many points of contrast between the Reformers and the Roman Catholic Church, which believes in original sin and in multiple effects of the fall but does not believe that our reason was in any way fatally impaired by the fall. Instead, the Roman Catholic Church teaches that the main effect of the fall was upon our senses. Therefore, for Roman Catholics, sensuality is the characteristic in which most persons see themselves as sinners. The Reformers believed, in contrast, that the Bible speaks clearly to the fact that there is an intellectual fall. The will now warps the intellect. The will is fallen and, therefore, produces a fallen reason.

The Reformers did not say that the reason was completely obliterated, any more than they said that the image of God was completely obliterated. If it were completely obliterated, we would not be able to have any kind of life. We would not have any kind of ordered civilization. Calvin went so far as to say that the heathens give us most of the sciences. We should not believe that our unregenerate neighbors know nothing. We all have been taught by unregenerate people. Reason is neither completely obliterated nor destroyed. Humanity is not irrational, but we are rationally given over to sin.

Like the Reformers, when we look at Scripture, we are drawn to make a distinction in our minds between natural knowledge and supernatural knowledge. Of course, an unregenerate person can know that two plus two equals four, find a cure to a disease, design a magnificent structure, or devise a technology that literally changes the world. However, when it comes to the most important issues of life, meaning, and questions about God and our soul—that is the point at which our reason is most corrupted. Leaning on Romans 1, the Reformers remind us that the unregenerate mind can never reason its way to salvation. The unregenerate mind will never reason its way to the cross. The cross is foolishness to Greeks. There is no way that we can find salvation in our intellect, because it is devastatingly fallen.

In 1 Corinthians 2:14, Paul writes, "The natural person does not accept the things of the Spirit of God, for they are folly to him, and he is not able to understand them because they are spiritually discerned." The unregenerate mind cannot understand regenerate things. It is not an educational problem; no amount of education can solve this problem. No manner of communication, illumination, seminars, classes, studies, or degrees will lead one to salvation, because the unregenerate reason is opposed to God. The unregenerate mind sees the gospel as foolishness and folly. For this reason, the apostle Paul himself was dismissed as an idle babbler. We see, again, the link between willing and knowing.

Fourteen Noetic Effects of the Fall

There are many facets of the daily intellectual life of human beings that are directly linked to the fall. While the noetic effects of the fall are inexhaustible, it is helpful to sketch out some of the ways in which they are noticeable.

1) Ignorance: had there been no fall, there would have been no ignorance. The things of God, even his invisible attributes, are clearly seen in creation, but the fall has clouded our ability to see these things. Ignorance would have been impossible until the fall, whereas it is now axiomatic.

2) Distractedness: every single human being has theological "attention deficit disorder." We are easily distracted.

3) Forgetfulness: everyone has committed to memory things that he has now forgotten. Forgetfulness would be impossible had we not sinned.

4) Prejudice: intellectual prejudice is one of our besetting problems. The problem is that we do not know ourselves well enough to know our intellectual prejudices, because we are prejudiced even in our thinking about our prejudices. One of the great achievements of

the postmodern mind-set has been the forcing of an honest discussion of intellectual prejudices.

5) Faulty perspective: because of our finitude, we all have a finite perspective on reality. Had we not sinned, we would all share a right and accurate perspective. As it is, we are shaped by cultural, linguistic, tribal, ethnic, historical, individual, familial, and other blinders. We do not see things as others see them, but we assume that others who are right-minded must see things as we see them. The famous "parable of the fish," often attributed to Aristotle, asks the question, "Does a fish know that it is wet?" The idea conveyed in the parable is that if you want to know what being wet is like, then do not ask a fish, for he does not know he is wet.

6) Intellectual fatigue: with the fast pace of modern life and the multitude of matters pressing for our attention, we can begin to feel depleted in our intellectual capacities and mental reserves.

7) Inconsistencies: it would be bad enough if we were merely plagued with inconsistencies. The bigger problem, however, is that we do not even see them in ourselves—though they are more readily detected by others.

8) Failure to draw the right conclusion: this is a besetting intellectual sin. Most people do not even recognize that they are drawing the wrong conclusions. There is the willful denial of and blindness toward data.

9) Intellectual apathy: if we did not bear the noetic effects of the fall, we would be infinitely passionate about the things that should be of our infinite concern. Our intellectual apathy, which works its way out in every dimension of our lives, is one of the most devastating effects of the fall.

10) Dogmatism and closed-mindedness: we hold to things with tenacity that we should not hold onto at all, because the intellect seizes upon certain ideas and thoughts like comfort food. They are only taken away from us with great force, even if reason and data directly contradict them.

11) Intellectual pride: the Scripture states that "'knowledge' puffs up" (1 Cor. 8:1). One danger of higher education is the besetting sin of human pride that comes alongside human achievement,

for intellectual achievements are some of the most highly prized trophies.

12) Vain imagination: Romans 1 indicts vain imagination, exposing the fact that we make images of God out of created things—even "birds and animals and creeping things" (v. 23). As the psalmist writes, "Why do the nations rage and the peoples plot in vain?" (Ps. 2:1).

13) Miscommunication: translation is difficult, and miscommunication is one of the great limitations upon intellectual advance. We live on the other side of both Genesis 3 (the fall) and Genesis 11 (confusion of language at Babel). From the story of the Tower of Babel, we understand that this issue of miscommunication is not an accident. Some of these noetic effects are because God has limited our knowledge.

14) Partial knowledge: we know only in part, and sometimes we do not even know how partial our knowledge is.

All of these noetic effects of the fall are tied to the will. These effects influence not only our intellectual activities but also the way our intellectual activities work their way out in other aspects of our lives—our emotions and intuitions. Human knowledge works in what might be called "intellectual auto-pilot." We operate the only way a sane person can operate. Our emotions and intuitions are shaped by our intellect, which is shaped by our will. As such, we find ourselves not always thinking in an openly rational, self-conscious way. Nonetheless, we remain driven by thinking that is working its way out in intuitions and emotions.

Thinking, Worldview, and Evangelism

Because of the intellectual devastation brought about by the fall, we are under obligation to think about thinking. That is why Christian discipleship is also an intellectual activity. We must come to terms with the fact that the noetic effects of the fall operate on multiple levels. The concern is that we rightly understand ourselves, and for that to happen, we must be told who we are and what our problem is. We are in desperate need of this knowledge.

We must also be concerned about understanding the natural mind. We must understand the unregenerate mind because of concern for reaching persons with the gospel of Jesus Christ. Missions and evangelism—indeed, the love we are to have for God and neighbor—compel us to seek to understand the unregenerate mind.

Over the last thirty or forty years, evangelicals have begun using a word that is borrowed from the Germans—*worldview*. This concept recognizes that the only way cognizant, aware human beings can operate is in a complex of thought that does not require us to rethink everything all at once, all the time. We operate out of a set of beliefs, principles, and axioms of thought that make sense of the world and allow us to make our way sensibly within it.

Sociologist Peter Berger refers to such things as "plausibility structures."[3] We inhabit a certain world that makes sense to us because we have certain habits of the mind that make the world plausible. Plausibility structures are quite important and absolutely basic. There have been some tremendous changes in plausibility structures over the course of Western civilization. The transitions from pre-modern to modern to postmodern reflect significant shifts that have taken place.

The odds are that you did not ask yourself before you got out of bed this morning whether or not you still believed in gravity. Believing in gravity is simply a part of your world picture. You did not worry about gravity—whether you were going to fall up out of bed. Neither did you wake up this morning in a deep existential crisis about whether you do or do not exist. Most human beings will experience such a crisis at some point in their life, but not every day. That is not the way we operate. If you had to think about things like gravity and your own existence every day, you would be immobilized.

We operate on the basic assumption that we exist. Likewise, we operate in a basic set of moral assumptions about what the good life is, what we are called to do, and what is right and wrong. We operate out of a certain sense of rationality, and we operate as economic people and political citizens. We function as neighbors, sons, daughters, husbands, and wives based on facts that we take for granted. The

---

[3]Peter L. Berger, *The Sacred Canopy: Elements of a Sociological Theory of Religion* (Garden City, NY: Doubleday, 1967).

problem is that worldviews show all the marks of human sinfulness just as every human culture, civilization, and soul does.

The Secular Mind

The natural mind that we are most likely to meet in this culture is a secular mind. *Secular* is a word that must be used carefully, because a secular mind is not necessarily a *fully* secularized mind. The prophets of the modern age believed that as human beings gained control over the great forces of nature, such as damming up rivers to create hydroelectricity or splitting the atom, and as the great mysteries gave way to knowledge given by scientific discovery, we would have less of a need for God. The great prophecy of secularization in the late eighteenth century and into the nineteenth and twentieth centuries was that Western civilization was going to become fully secularized. This has not happened, at least not in North America.

In Western Europe, however, total secularization is almost complete. Current estimates are that only between three and four percent of most persons in Belgium, the Netherlands, France, and many other countries actually attend church on a regular basis. Despite the presence of the great cathedrals, the European mind has been almost fully secularized. This is a geographical distinction, however, because 80 to 90 percent of North Americans say they believe in God, and at least 70 percent of Americans darken the door of some church each year. In addition, 55 percent of Americans say they go to church at least three out of four weeks.

Sociologists show that secularization is not only geographically distinct, but that class also is a distinguishing factor. It turns out that in American higher education, the secularization thesis has worked its way out in similar fashion to Europe. That is to say, the most secularized cohort of the American population primarily contains those who have tenure in American universities. The cultural creatives, especially those involved in the arts and the media, tend to be far more secular than even the others are. The ruling elites, to use a sociological category, tend to be pervasively secularized. Peter Berger discussed a longitudinal study that sought to determine which cultures were the most religious and the least religious. The study revealed that the least religious people in the world are Swedes, whereas the most religious people in the world are in India. Peter Berger then described the United States as a nation of Indians ruled by an elite of Swedes.[4] The thing that must be understood, however, is that the secular mind is not necessarily an unreligious mind. It may be irreligious, but it is not unreligious. The secular mind ordinarily has some object of ultimate fidelity and concern.

Five Precepts of the Modern Mind

In order to understand better the modern mind, consider these five precepts. First, the modern mind is characterized by *postmodern anti-realism*. There are people in American society who are not sure that what we are talking about is even real. They argue that the terms of morality—statements about what is right and wrong—are merely a language game.

The second precept is *moral relativism*. Although most of the people we know do not actually hold to anti-realism, it has filtered down into the culture as moral relativism. Most unregenerate Americans today are selective moral relativists. A recent study suggested that the moral issue on which there has been the greatest change in America over the last forty years is premarital sex.[5] In 1970, 80 percent of Americans believed that premarital sex was wrong. In 2010, however, only 20 percent believe it is wrong. What accounts for this radical shift in moral belief? One reason for the shift is the abandonment of a worldview that believes in the existence of right and wrong.

Third, there is *therapeutic universalism*. In our day, the natural mind has adopted a worldview that espouses the motto, "You are either in therapy, or you are in denial." The idea is that our basic problems will be solved by therapy.

The fourth precept is *radical pluralism*. In one sense, pluralism is just a fact—there are people with a plurality of worldviews around

---

[4]Peter Berger, Grace Davie, Effie Fokas, *Religious America, Secular Europe? A Theme and Variations* (London: Ashgate, 2008), 12.
[5]*When Marriage Disappears: The New Middle America*, The State of Our Unions 2010, The National Marriage Project, University of Virginia (December 2010). The full report, along with other materials and an executive summary are available at http://stateofourunions.org/.

us. Pluralism is also an ideology, however, suggesting that there is no one worldview that can be correct.

The fifth precept is *managerial pragmatism*. We live in the midst of people who genuinely believe that most problems can be managed. The goal here is not to solve problems so much as to manage them through procedural democracy.

Three Operating Conditions of Belief

The unregenerate mind is the unregenerate mind. The natural mind is the natural mind. Although it does not change from Genesis 3 until Jesus comes, it does put on different clothing. The Canadian philosopher Charles Taylor provides us with something very helpful in his massive book *A Secular Age*, as he argues that there have been three operating conditions of belief in Western civilization.[6]

Explaining the first condition, Taylor writes about an age when disbelief in God was impossible. The word *atheist* did not exist in the English language until the time of Queen Elizabeth. There was not even a word for it, because atheism was not an available category. The only way you could explain how the world worked was in reference to God. One might have argued about which god was God or whose God was right, but one did not argue about whether there was a God or not.

Then, he discusses the modern era, the Enlightenment, the rise of modern science, and all that these movements entailed. Taylor argues that there arose a second condition of belief, involving the possibility of disbelief. It is a significant shift to move from an impossibility of disbelief to a possibility of disbelief.

Finally, although there is no precise dividing line, many persons in the present day have moved into the third condition—the impossibility of belief. As we go about our everyday tasks as Christians, engaging in the world in which the Lord has put us, we will run up against many people for whom belief in God seems to be impossible. That is one mark of the current dress of the natural mind. Most people, however, especially those who are not primarily involved in higher education, remain in the former two categories.

---

[6]Charles Taylor, *A Secular Age* (Cambridge, MA: Belknap Press of Harvard University, 2007).

Twelve Features of the Natural Mind

Consider these twelve precepts as a way of understanding the current clothing of the natural mind. They are encapsulated as spoken words or mottos, a shorthand manner of describing each of them.

The first feature is, "I am who I think I am." The natural mind declares, "I define who I am, I know who I am, and I have the power to look in the mirror and within myself in order to discover who I am. If I change my thinking about who I am, I will change who I am."

Second, "I may do some bad things, but I am not a bad person." The contemporary dress of the natural mind is not undiluted moral relativism, but the kind that maintains that the individual is relatively more moral than the people around him are. For example, an article by a business professor who caught students cheating relayed that every single one of the students maintained that they knew it was a bad thing, but each one said, "This is not me." He responded aptly, "Yes, it is, evidently; you are the one who did it."

Third, "Something is wrong, but it is not my fault." It is almost universally known by individuals that there is something wrong with their life. There is awareness that they have a need, yet they think that it is not their fault. They are not liable for whatever it is that has gone wrong.

Fourth, "Something happened to me." This is logically prior to the previous feature. The natural mind, in its modern dress, is looking for the new book or the new seminar to explain what happened. The latest *Diagnostic and Statistical Manual of Mental Disorders*, the manual of diagnosis for the psychiatric and psychological professions that is even now being put together, is one of the most controversial things in the psychological world. What should, or should not, be considered a "mental disorder"? By the time it is finished, everyone is going to be in there.

Fifth, "Morality is a good idea, but it is relatively relative." As the cultural conversation continues, one can see absolute certainty that some things are wrong yet has a hesitancy to declare that other things are wrong. The list changes frequently and swiftly. For instance, in almost any setting, prostitution has been considered wrong—at least until very recently. Now, the province of Ontario has legalized prostitution.[7] They claimed that they did so because they wanted to make it safer.

Sixth, "What goes around comes around." This is American karma. It is not the hard-line Confucian kind of karma, but a vague notion that people get what they deserve.

Seventh, "There is not only one way of anything. Period."

Eighth, "God is available as an explanation when needed." When you do not have an answer, then perhaps God will suffice.

Ninth, "God is available as a helper in case of emergency."

Tenth, "Science or technology will solve most big problems." This is the genuine belief that modern medicine, psychiatry, and more will be able to solve most problems.

Eleventh, "I may need help, but I can negotiate the terms."

Twelfth, "Most people are well intended, but some people are just mean."

The Frontline Intellectual Crisis of Our Day

Sociologist Christian Smith and his associates did a massive survey in which they interviewed well over 3,000 people about their beliefs. The study revealed that the basic faith of Americans is what they call "moralistic therapeutic deism."[8] Most people believe that God wants them to have a loosely defined goodness, to feel good about themselves, and to be healthy and whole. This is, in effect, deism. They believe there is a god, but he is not a god who is intimately involved in their lives. Although he is not a god who rules over the universe, he nonetheless remains an important cultural referent. This study is the most accurate indictment of the unregenerate American mind's cultural dress at the present. The people Smith was surveying, however, were not mass Americans and secular culture. They were adolescents and young adults in our churches. Therefore, this is the frontline of the intellectual crisis of our day.

We must think about thinking, because if we are not intellectual disciples of Jesus Christ, we will find the natural mind staring us in

---

[7]Michael Foust, "Canadian Court OKs Legalized Prostitution," *Baptist Press*, October 6, 2010.

[8]Christian Smith and Melina Lundquist Denton, *Soul Searching: The Religious and Spiritual Lives of American Teenagers* (Oxford: Oxford University Press, 2005); also, *Souls in Transition: The Religious and Spiritual Lives of Emerging Adults* (Oxford: Oxford University Press, 2009).

the face. Because of our own intuitions and reflexes, when those who believe the gospel are put under intellectual pressure, it is very easy to be inconsistent. Therefore, if as Christians we are going to think in a way that honors God, we must first avail ourselves constantly of the Word of God. Secondly, we must avail ourselves constantly of the life of the local church. Third, we must depend constantly upon the corrective presence of the Holy Spirit in our lives to conform us to the image of Christ.

At the end of the day, we are not smarter than the rest. We are not morally superior to those who do not know Christ. We did not come to know salvation in Christ because we are wise. Salvation is all of grace. Our intellectual discipleship must be demonstrated in the renewing of our minds—by the word and through the Spirit and in the church.

Keep thinking—until Jesus comes.

* * *

Dear Heavenly Father,
We thank you for giving us the gift of minds. We know that you gave us this gift in order that we might know you and find our greatest joy in thinking about you. Forgive us our many intellectual sins. For allowing our minds to think thoughts unworthy of you, for thinking thoughts of rebellion rather than obedience, evil rather than good, doubt rather than faith. Forgive us our forgetfulness, our wandering minds, our short attention spans, and our wayward imaginations.

Thank you for redeeming our minds in Christ, and for imparting your Spirit within us for the renewal of our minds. Redeem our patterns of thinking that we will think rightly, obediently, and humbly. Give us imaginations guided by the Scriptures, awe as we worship you with our minds, and conviction in order to share the gospel of Jesus Christ with others.

Create in us a pure mind, oh Lord, and train our intellects in the school of your Word.
Amen

3

Thinking Deeply in the Ocean of Revelation:

The Bible and the Life of the Mind

R. C. SPROUL

In the book of Acts, Luke's magnificent account of the spread of the gospel in the early church, we read of a particularly interesting encounter between the apostle Paul and a gathering of pagan philosophers in that capital of ancient philosophy, Athens. The encounter is recorded for us in Acts 17, where we read:

> Now while Paul was waiting for them at Athens, his spirit was provoked within him as he saw that the city was full of idols. So he reasoned in the synagogue with the Jews and the devout persons, and in the marketplace every day with those who happened to be there. Some of the Epicurean and Stoic philosophers also conversed with him. And some said, "What does this babbler wish to say?" Others said, "He seems to be a preacher of foreign divinities"—because he was preaching Jesus and the resurrection. And they took him and brought him to the Areopagus, saying, "May we know what this new teaching is that you are presenting? For you bring some strange things to our ears. We wish to know therefore what these things mean." Now all the Athenians and the foreigners who lived there would spend their time in nothing except telling or hearing something new.

So Paul, standing in the midst of the Areopagus, said: "Men of Athens, I perceive that in every way you are very religious. For as I passed along and observed the objects of your worship, I found also an altar with this inscription, 'To the unknown god.' What therefore you worship as unknown, this I proclaim to you. The God who made the world and everything in it, being Lord of heaven and earth, does not live in temples made by man, nor is he served by human hands, as though he needed anything, since he himself gives to all mankind life and breath and everything. And he made from one man every nation of mankind to live on all the face of the earth, having determined allotted periods and the boundaries of their dwelling place, that they should seek God, in the hope that they might feel their way toward him and find him. Yet he is actually not far from each one of us, for 'In him we live and move and have our being'; as even some of your own poets have said, 'For we are indeed his offspring.'" (Acts 17:16–28)

The Problem of Ultimate Reality

Centuries before Paul's visit to Athens, there lived in the city of Miletus a man named Thales, who today is often acknowledged as the father not only of Western philosophy but also of Western science. The word *science* originally meant "knowledge." The task of the scientist and the task of the philosopher—even the task of the theologian—is to pursue knowledge wherever it may be found and whatever the consequences of that search may be.

Thales was captivated by a pressing problem about which all thinking people in the ancient world were concerned. The question was this: "How can I make sense of all of the diversity of my experience in this world? I see a variety of things. I see trees, horses, bushes, people, the moon, the stars, and myriad other things in their vast variety. How do they all fit together? How can I have a coherent or unified sense of my knowledge and of my experience?"

In other words, the quest was for a "universe." The word *universe* is a hybrid term. It comes from the combination of two distinct words—the word *unity* and the word *diversity*. This was the goal that preoccupied Thales and others like him. They wanted to find the unity that would make sense of all of the diversity they experienced. So Thales was trying to solve the problem of what we call unity and diversity, the problem of the one and the many, in order to have an intelligible understanding of the world.

Cosmos, Not Chaos

Some of you will recall the 1980 television series hosted by Carl Sagan, *Cosmos*, which led to a book by the same title. In the first episode of that series, and on the first page of his book, Sagan made the observation that scientists are searching to understand a reality that can be understood, that is, "cosmos," not "chaos." If all we had were undifferentiated sensory experiences with nothing to tie them together, no principle of unity or coherence, we would have chaos, not cosmos. Finding that cosmos was Sagan's goal, and it was Thales's goal as well. He was looking for the ultimate reality, the single *archae* or chief principle that would explain everything in existence. More specifically, he was concerned to find explanations for ultimate reality, for life, and for motion.

All Is Water (Thales)

You may be amused when you hear the answers Thales found. In the first instance, he came to the conclusion that ultimate reality, the singular principle that makes sense of everything else in this world, is water. Imagine today a philosopher or a scientist saying that all reality has coherence and makes sense because fundamentally all reality is a form of water. Why did Thales come to this conclusion? He noticed that everything he saw in the world appeared in one of three forms. It was either a solid, a liquid, or a gas. That understanding led him to look for some element that had the ability to manifest itself in all three of these forms. The perfect answer was water, because it appears as water in its liquid form, as ice in its solid form, and as steam in its gaseous form. Since water has this ability to appear in all three forms, Thales concluded that it must be the ultimate reality that makes up everything.

The Problem of Life

Then he asked the next question: What explains the question of life, its origin, its significance, its power? Again, Thales came to water, because he noticed that in order for anything to live, as we understand life, it required the nourishment gained from water. Human beings perish in a short time if they are deprived of water. You know what happens to your grass or your flowers when drought comes and the water source dries up—these plants perish. Thales concluded that the power of life must be invested in water.

The Problem of Motion

But there was another question that Thales found befuddling as a philosopher and a scientist, a problem that plagued all the ancient thinkers. It was the problem of motion. How can we explain motion? When we look around ourselves, if we see anything that is moving, we conclude that it is being moved by something else. Stones don't get off the ground and throw themselves through the air. Somebody has to pick up the stone and throw it. The pool ball remains motionless on the table until somebody takes a cue stick and hits the cue ball against the object ball in order to get the movement going for a pool game to take place. And there is not much fun in golf if the ball never moves, if the club is never swung. So Thales arrived at a primitive understanding of inertia—the theory that later was refined to say that bodies that are at rest tend to remain at rest unless acted upon by an outward force, and bodies in motion tend to stay in motion unless they are acted upon by an outside force.

Incidentally, this is still a problem for advocates for the big bang theory of cosmology, who postulate that for all eternity all of reality was in a state of absolute organization, with all matter and energy compressed into an infinitesimal singularity—until one Thursday afternoon at two o'clock, the thing exploded. They want to explain that, of course, without the intrusion of an outside force.

I once had some correspondence with Dr. Sagan about this very question. I asked him, "How do you account for the change from that eternal inert state?" His answer was simply this: "Well, I really don't want to go there. I don't think we can go further back than to the billionth of a microsecond before the big bang, and before that it is a mystery." I said: "You're a scientist. You have to ask why the change occurred."

Hylozoism

As Thales wrestled with this question, he looked for something that had the capacity for hylozoism. *Hylozoism* was an ancient word similar to our word *automobile*. An automobile is called an automobile because, when it is performing the way it is supposed to, it has the ability to move itself. In the ancient world, hylozoism was the belief that life resides in all matter, giving it the ability to move without being pushed, pulled, thrown, or otherwise induced by an outside force. As Thales studied this question, he came to the conclusion that water is the primary hylozoistic substance, the essence of all matter, because if we observe water, we see oceans, tides, and waves rolling onto the shore, and rivers and streams flowing, but we do not see anyone causing the motion. Of course, Thales was not aware of the gravitational pull of the moon and the cause of tides that we understand in our modern perspective.

So for Thales, water seemed to solve the problem of ultimate reality, the problem of life, and the problem of motion. He thought he had reached the end of philosophical inquiry, but those who followed after him suggested other alternatives. They included men such as Anaximander, Anaximenes, and Anaxagoras. But ultimately the two most important philosophers who came along before Plato and Aristotle were Parmenides and Heraclitus, and they wrestled principally with the same questions Thales had examined.

"Whatever Is, Is"

Parmenides, whose works have all but vanished from the face of the earth except for a few fragments that have been discovered, was famous for his profound statement "Whatever is, is." When I was a student in college, a professor very soberly made the announcement in the classroom that Parmenides had declared, "Whatever is, is." I remember thinking, "And this fellow is famous?" But in time, through my study of philosophy, I realized I have never heard anything with deeper significance or greater profundity than this observation by Parmenides.

What was he getting at? He was saying that if something is real, it cannot not be. Nonbeing is nothingness. Nothingness has no onto-logical status. It simply is not. Parmenides said that for anything to exist, there has to be something that is pure, unchanging, immutable, fully actualized being, something that has no potential left to be real-ized. As Aristotle would observe later, that which is fully actual has no potential, and that which is only potential has no actuality. So if a thing, a person, or an object has nothing but potential, that person would not exist at all.

"Whatever Is, Is Changing"

Over against the thinking of Parmenides was that of the philosopher Heraclitus, who many regard as the ancient father of modern exis-tential philosophy. Heraclitus, instead of saying, "Whatever is, is," made the assertion, "Whatever is, is changing." Everything that we experience in the world in which we live is undergoing change. It is going through some kind of mutation. We all experience change con-stantly, if only in the experience of aging. I am a day older today than I was yesterday. The cells within my body are undergoing change as a result of that aging process. There is growth and decay all around us. So the operative word to describe the reality that we experience, according to Heraclitus, is *change*, or, as he called it, *flux*. Everything, he said, is in a state of flux.

Heraclitus was famous for saying, "You can't step into the same river twice." Why? Because before you can take a second step, the river has moved on; it has changed—with your second step you place your foot into an entirely different set of water molecules. Not only has the river changed, but also the riverbed has changed. It may be nothing more than a microscopic step in the process of erosion that no one can see with the naked eye. Nevertheless, it has taken place. But not only have the river and the riverbed changed; you have changed. So change or mutation is the chief characteristic of everything that we experience.

Thus, Heraclitus came to the conclusion, "Whatever is, is chang-ing." There is nothing that is; there is only that which is changing. So the distinction was then made between pure being that does not change and that which does change, which we call *becoming*.

Whatever you are in this instant is not what you will be an hour from now. You are becoming something different from what you are at this very moment. You cannot freeze the moment; it is past. In reality, you are not a human being but a human becoming.

Skepticism and the Impasse between *Being* and *Becoming*

This impasse between Parmenides and Heraclitus produced a spirit of cynicism and skepticism in ancient culture. People decided that if these two intellectual giants could not figure out the distinction between being and becoming, unity and diversity, then the scientific enterprise was doomed. The whole quest for ultimate truth and ultimate reality must be a fool's errand. The skeptics stepped onto the stage and said we really cannot have any lasting or significant knowledge. Knowledge itself is impossible. Everything is relative. There are no absolutes.

Both Are Necessary (Socrates, Plato, and Aristotle)

Then a certain gadabout in Athens started disturbing the skeptics by asking them penetrating questions and driving them to different conclusions. His name was Socrates, and his most famous student was Plato. Socrates said we cannot have a coherent view of science, of philosophy, or of any kind of knowledge itself unless we account both for being and for becoming. He believed both are necessary. A coherent philosophy, a coherent science, must have both unity and diversity.

So Plato constructed his massive theory of ideas in order to solve this problem, but he was left with a few difficulties that his most famous student sought to resolve. His name was Aristotle. Even though Aristotle came to a different conclusion from his master, Plato, he was driven by the same issues—being and becoming, unity and diversity. Aristotle said that there has to be a being who is the source of all motion, but who is not the result of someone else's motion. So he postulated that the first or ultimate cause is God, as it were, whom he called the Unmoved Mover.

If there have been any real titans of philosophy and science, they were Plato and Aristotle. In fact, Aristotle's nickname to this day is *"the* philosopher." Contemporary scholars have said that all philosophical inquiry since Plato and Aristotle amounts to mere footnotes to the work of those two men. In the centuries that have come and gone since Plato and Aristotle, the questions have not significantly changed. Philosophers are still seeking to unravel the conundrum of metaphysics, of being. We are still baffled in many ways by the mystery of life. Scientists are offering rewards for fully intelligible explanations of motion and all of its intricacies. So Plato and Aristotle did not resolve these questions. In fact, when Plato and Aristotle could not come to an agreement, a new wave of skepticism swept over ancient Greece and brought forth the minor philosophical schools of the Stoics and the Epicureans.

Another Wave of Skepticism (Stoics and Epicureans)

The Stoics and the Epicureans were archrivals. They disagreed fundamentally about many points of philosophy and of psychology. But they were both equally skeptical about the ability of the human mind to come to a final conclusion as to the ultimate questions. So in a real sense, they abandoned the quest for ultimate reality, for ultimate truth, and turned their attention to things they could learn, things that they could use right away.

Though they were different in many ways, the Epicureans and the Stoics were both trying to answer the same question: How can I live in this world and be happy? In other words, how can I have peace in my mind, in my soul? Their quest was for *adorakia*. You probably have never heard the word *adorakia* unless you have taken a tranquilizer that has that brand name on it, but in ancient Greek the word *adorakia* meant freedom from oppression and anxiety. It had to do with gaining what the Stoics called "a sense of imperturbability."

The Epicureans were radical hedonists. Hedonism is defined by the pursuit of pleasure and the avoidance of pain. The Epicureans would have banquets, gorging themselves with food, and then would induce themselves to vomit so they could eat more. They would drink until they were stumbling drunk, then they would vomit and drink some more. They engaged in orgies with unlimited sex to get as much pleasure as they could endure. But soon they discovered what has been called the hedonistic paradox, the truth that if your desires are not met, you become frustrated, and if they are met, you become bored. So, few Epicureans ended up satisfied with that lifestyle. That's why the Stoics came up with a calculus, as it were, to balance the ledger. They said you must have just the right amount of gluttony, just the right amount of drunkenness, and just the right amount of sexual activity so that you could avoid the clutches of the hedonistic paradox.

Thankfully, John Piper has rescued the word *hedonism* and has taught us about spiritual hedonism, godly hedonism.[1] He understands the foundational principles of our humanity as it was created by God, the truth that we will never be fully satisfied, we will never discover ultimate pleasure, until we find it in God himself. This is the pleasure we should be seeking with all our being.

The Apostle Paul Comes to Athens

Let's return now to the apostle Paul. He came for the first time to Athens, the cultural center of the ancient world, the city of Socrates, of Plato, of Aristotle, of so many great minds of the ancient world within the fields of medicine, political theory, philosophy, astronomy, and mathematics. But since the advent of skepticism, the golden age had been tarnished, and Athens had become a different kind of city. When Paul saw it for the first time, as Luke tells us, he was deeply moved, not by its art, not by its medicine, not by its political structures, but because he saw that the city was given totally to idolatry. The city had become a factory devoted to the manufacturing of pagan idols. When he saw that, Paul was moved to action.

He went to the synagogue. He went to the agora, the marketplace. And wherever he went, he preached Jesus and the resurrection from the dead. It was there that he encountered some Epicureans and Stoics, and they took him up to the Areopagus, to Mars Hill, within sight of the agora and the Parthenon, and there on that small mesa, as it were, he conversed with these philosophers whose practice it was to meet every day to discuss what was new.

---

[1]See John Piper, *Desiring God: Meditations of a Christian Hedonist*, 4th ed. (Colorado Springs, CO: Multnomah, 2011).

Intoxicated with Novelty

People have always been intoxicated with novelty. In our day, we have the Internet or the television news networks to tell us what's new. In earlier times, people relied on the newspapers. You can still buy a newspaper on the corner, but it will not have the latest news. Plus, if you put in your coins and open the box only to find yesterday's newspaper, it is worthless. Nobody cares about yesterday's newspaper. We want to hear the latest news.

There may be no group of people more addicted to novelty than theologians. I was recently interviewed by a newspaper in Orlando. One of the things the newspaper reporter observed about me is that I teach and preach a "throwback theology." What in the world is a throwback theology? I guess he thought it was a theology that ought to be thrown back rather than kept. In other words, he felt that this theologian was out of touch with contemporary views and theology. He saw me as stuck in the mud with classical, biblical theology while other theologians are more progressive.

The philosophers Paul encountered two thousand years ago in Athens were just as interested in hearing something new as we are today. So Paul took advantage of that and began to teach them, and he said, while he was standing on the Areopagus, "Men of Athens, I perceive that in every way you are very religious" (v. 22).

I was once invited to speak at a Christian college in the Midwest that was without a president, and the staff had been engaging in a self-study before calling a new executive. They asked me to address the faculty and the administration on the subject "What is a Christian college?" Before I spoke, they gave me a tour of the campus, through the class buildings, the science hall, the student union, and the faculty office building. I noticed that one of the doors had a small sign that said "Department of Religion." I was a bit surprised by that. So that evening, when I addressed the faculty, I said, "Today I was observing your campus, and I see that you have a Department of Religion. Was it always called the department of religion?" Most of them looked at me with blank stares, but an elderly faculty member in the back of the room raised his hand and said: "No, no, no. When I first came to this campus, it was the Department of Theology, but many, many years ago we changed it to the Department of Religion." When I asked him why it was changed, he said, "I'm not sure, but I think the main reason was so that our students could transfer their credits to secular universities without difficulty." I went on to point out that, as I understand the divisions of academic investigation, the study of theology is the study of God. The study of religion should be underneath anthropology or sociology, because the study of religion is the study of human beings and how they behave with whatever they regard as sacred or cultic.

Religious and Far Away from God

A person can be extremely religious and yet be as far away from God as it is possible to be. That was the situation of the Athenians, and Paul noticed. He said, "You people are filled with religion." He could say that because he had seen their idols everywhere he went in Athens. And just in case they had missed a god, they had an altar devoted to "the unknown god" (v. 23). They were hedging their bets. When W. C. Fields was dying in a hospital, one of his friends came to see him and found him reading the Bible. The friend was shocked because Fields was anything but a religious man. He said, "W. C., what are you doing?" Fields replied, "I'm looking for a loophole." That's what the Greeks were doing.

To an Unknown God

Paul used their altar to an unknown god as a jumping-off point to tell them that the one whom they were worshiping in ignorance was the same God he had been sent to proclaim, the one who is the creator of all. He does not need prayers, gifts, or worship. In fact, he does not need anything. He is Lord of heaven and earth. He does not live in temples made by men. He is not served by human hands. Instead, he gives to all men life and breath and everything. He made every nation of mankind from one man, and then determined the periods and boundaries of their dwellings. Then Paul urged the Athenian philosophers to seek God in the hope that they might feel their way to him and find him, for God is actually not far from each one of us (vv. 24–27).

We Exist, Live, and Move in God

Then Paul gave what may be the most profound philosophical statement anywhere in the New Testament. Quoting pagan philosophers, he said of God, "In him we live and move and have our being" (v. 28).

Did you hear that, Thales? Ultimate reality is found in God and only in God, who is the creator of everything. He is an absolutely pure being. He reveals himself to Moses in the Midianite wilderness by the memorial name, "I AM WHO I AM" (Ex. 3:14). He alone eternally is. He alone is pure actuality. What is God's potential? How can the Lord get any better? He is already perfect.

When I was playing golf recently, I hit my tee shot on a par-three hole, saw that it was going right to the flag, and didn't see it land. My partner said, "You hit a perfect shot. It's right next to the hole." Then it wasn't a perfect shot. There was room for improvement. But with God, there is no room for improvement. He is pure being and ultimate reality. The only hope for finding unity in the diversity of this world is in his perfect being.

I'm a human being. More accurately, I'm a human becoming. I still have potential that has not yet been realized. I'm changing. I'm undergoing mutations. That is the chief characteristic of creaturely existence—mutability. We change. But God does not. That means my being is not found in me independently. None of us created ourselves. All of us are dependent on something before us to account for our very existence.

Where do we find the power of that life? Not in water. It is found in God, who alone brings something out of nothing. He brings life out of death, for he is the God of resurrection. That is why Paul was addressing the Athenians about Jesus and his resurrection. He was talking to them about the ultimate answer to life, which is found in God and in his resurrected Son.

When it comes to motion, the universe cannot move without the providential power of God. The only thing that is hylozoistic in the ultimate sense is God himself. Our power to move is secondary. We have no primary causal power. Primary causal power belongs to God and to God alone.

The Bible Gives the Ultimate Answers

I hope you can see from this brief introduction that biblical revelation gives to us the answers to the ultimate and persistent questions that have plagued the quest of theoretical thought as long as there have been people. We will never find an explanation for being, for life, or for motion if we try to find it outside the being and the character of God.

*   *   *

Almighty God and Heavenly Father,
We praise and extol you, the maker of heaven and earth, the fountain of being, the source and sustainer of life—the one whose glory the heavens declare. Thank you for revealing yourself, and ultimate reality, through your Word. Your Word is truth—sanctify us by this truth. Now as we study your Word, may it reveal to us the Word-made-flesh, Jesus Christ, who, through his righteous obedience and atoning work on the cross, brings us back to you—to whom be everlasting glory and praise.
Amen

4

Thinking for the Sake of Global Faithfulness:

Encountering Islam with the Mind of Christ

THABITI ANYABWILE

The fullest expression of Christian living is a combination of head, heart, and hands. It involves receiving truth through the head, which ignites new affections in the heart and flows out in action through the hands.

There is an increasing anti-intellectualism and mindless entertainment built on stereotype when it comes to Islam and Muslims. Have you noticed in the popular mediums of television and film how twenty years ago the bad guys were always the "Red Soviet threat"? But now you cannot watch a sitcom or drama without "Arab Muslim terrorists" featured as the bad guys.

How We Commonly Feel and Talk about Islam

Along with that shift in imagery comes a shift to adversarial language that creates a posture of at least skepticism and often hostility. We use combative words and phrases such as "the threat of Islam," "clash of civilization," "extremists," and "confrontation."

Along with these popular cultural expressions and images, you may hear certain frequently asked questions such as, "How do I witness to Muslims?" and "What should we do about Islam?" Beneath these questions are assumptions that Muslims are unreachable or are perhaps the most unreasonable of all people.

Underlying both the anti-intellectual and mindless entertainment as well as the frequently asked questions is one basic emotion: fear. A lot of us are afraid of Muslims and Islam. Perhaps as we walk about our neighborhoods or shopping malls and see people dressed in Muslim clothing, we have noticed in ourselves a skepticism, a hesitancy or pulling back in our hearts. It's fear. And where fear takes control, thinking does not.

We notice all kinds of typical responses triggered by fear. For example, we see fear manifested in "fight" responses. Think of the verbal sparring in the summer of 2010 over the proposed mosque at Ground Zero. At other times, fear surfaces as a "flight" response. Perhaps our lack of zeal in evangelism and missions simply reflects our running in fear from Muslim neighbors. Or, in fear some simply accommodate or acquiesce. Sometimes the fear is manifested in plain, ugly hatred.

Thinking for Global Faithfulness

But we are called to be thinking people, especially as Christians. We are called to love the Lord our God with all our mind, all our intellect, in the cause of being faithful to God and enjoying him forever.

Thinking, very simply, is using one's mind rationally in the evaluation of a subject or situation. It is to develop or have a belief, opinion, or judgment of something.

Thinking is not the same as reacting. And perhaps nowhere is it more important to distinguish between solid, rich, deep thinking and reacting than in our consideration of Islam.

Thinking is not sloganeering. We can't be said to be thinking people if all we're really doing is parroting favorite quips and phrases and positions on things we have not thought through. Talk of "clash of civilizations" may make for provocative phraseology, but it does little to help us think.

Thinking is not stereotyping. A stereotype is a really efficient way to simplify complexity. Stereotypes tend to reduce vast amounts

Bad Pluralism

But, on the other hand, there also exists what we might call an uncritical, unthinking, even naïve pluralism. This is the kind of pluralism, multiculturalism, or diversity seeking that fails to distinguish between the inherent worth of people made in God's image and ideas. There's a difference between valuing people as equal and valuing ideas as though every idea is equal in worth. Not all ideas are created equal. Failing to remember this is the first mistake we make in our thinking when encountering religious perspectives, including Islam.

We see an example of this in the kind of religious pluralism that says, "All religions are true and all are beautiful." Or, "All roads lead to God. All religions are climbing the same mountain." Those comments reflect a naïve pluralism.

What makes this approach to pluralism naïve and unhelpful? First, this approach to pluralism *flattens differences*—real and significant differences—that matter to the practitioners of various religions or cultural views. There is a cultural tendency to downplay anything that divides or differentiates.

Therefore, second, this kind of naïve pluralism *proves ethically irresponsible* because it doesn't address real social problems and challenges occasioned by the diversity of our world. While a pluralistic society offers benefits, it also poses challenges stemming from the same diversity. We ignore these differences at significant risk to the true well-being and peace of society. We live in a world where failing to understand real and significant differences leads to car bombs, plane hijackings, bullets flying, and civil wars.

Third, a naïve pluralism is unhelpful because it *fails to account for the far-reaching effects of diversity*. In most cultures, diversity influences nearly every aspect of society. For example, religious diversity alone impacts everything from economics (no-interest banking among Arab Muslims), to politics (evangelical voting blocks in American elections), to military and war (Protestant and Catholic "troubles" in Northern Ireland).

To understand our world, we have to understand something about the differences among people—especially religious differences.

As Stephen Prothero puts it, "Even if religion makes no sense to you, you need to make sense of religions to make sense of the world."[1] A naïve pluralism turns us into ostriches with our heads buried beneath the sand and our rear ends in the air, hoping no one will see us and harm us. It's not a thinking posture.

My three-year-old son, Titus, likes to play hide-and-seek while we're driving in the car. He throws his favorite blanket over his head and calls, "Dad, you can't find me." His legs dangle exposed beneath the blanket, but he thinks he's hidden and safe. I like to reach back and gently pluck him in the forehead as he giggles. So much of our engagement with people not like us reminds me of Titus cowering beneath his blanket while exposed.

Why Does Naïve Pluralism Take Root in Society?

But if a naïve pluralism is so bad, then why does it find support in our culture? What causes it to grow in our society? There are at least six reasons. Understanding these reasons helps us to see why engaging Islam in a naïvely pluralistic context is fraught with so many difficulties.[2]

1) *We have become uncomfortable with argument.* Prothero helpfully points out, "The ideal of religious tolerance has morphed into religious agreement."[3] We hear people say, as if it is a superior virtue, "I never talk about politics and religion." When you hear someone say that, realize you may have a talking ostrich expressing his or her discomfort with disagreement and argument.

2) *There is a readiness to blur the significant differences in the major goals of religion.* Christians customarily think that every religion has personal salvation as its main aim. But not every religion maintains the same goal for its religious practice. To illustrate this point, Prothero offers a helpful multiple-choice question: Which sport is best at producing runs: basketball, football, hockey, or baseball?

[1]Stephen Prothero, *God Is Not One: The Eight Rival Religions That Run the World—And Why Their Differences Matter* (New York: HarperOne, 2010), 8.
[2]For good discussions of religious pluralism and associated problems, see the introductory essay in Prothero, *God Is Not One*, 1–24; and Harold A. Netland and Keith E. Johnson, "Why Is Religious Pluralism Fun—and Dangerous?" in *Telling the Truth: Evangelizing Postmoderns*, ed. D. A. Carson (Grand Rapids, MI: Zondervan, 2002), 47–67.
[3]Prothero, *God Is Not One*, 4.

The obvious answer is baseball. Why? Because "runs" are not the goal in other sports; "runs" only make sense in baseball. So it is with religious ideals. If we are to understand and engage other religious perspectives, we will need to resist a naïve pluralism that fails to ask, "What is the major goal of this or that religion or cultural practice?" All religions are not seeking the same goal or, to use the popular expression, climbing the same mountain. They are not even pretending to do so. Not all religions are motivated by the goal of salvation from sin and wrath. In fact, salvation is a distinctively Christian concept.

3) *There is a tendency to avoid the big questions in life*. We are amusing ourselves to death. We do not want to ponder questions such as: Why are we here? Where are we going? How are we to live? Does God exist? Does evil exist? Do we exist? So, naïve pluralism becomes a grand pact in avoidance and finds a comfortable home in a culture that doesn't want to face big questions.

4) *The culture emphasizes subjective privatism and sincerity*. The highest ideals are all tailor-made to the individual and protected by a privacy fence. Sincerity and undiscriminating tolerance matter most, not facts and final judgments. We live in a culture that prizes preferences over propositions.

5) *The naïve pluralist regards religion in highly pragmatic, consumerist terms*. Consequently, the major questions are: "What works for me?" "What do I want to purchase with my time and resources?" The consumer is always right, even if he cobbles together bits and pieces of various religious perspectives and tastes over truth. For that reason, the culture silences rigorous thinking and discussion about differences. So, a religious pragmatism motivates behavior and decisions.

6) *The naïve pluralist, therefore, does not prize universals, absolutes, or superlatives*. Asking, "Which religion is true?" becomes off-limits. Fundamentals and absolutes receive harsh rejection. Such a pluralist embraces a kind of perspectivalism[4] that views truth from a personal vantage point. Think of the old story of three blind men

---

[4]Not to be confused with the multiperspectival (and triperspectival) framework found in writings of John M. Frame and Vern S. Poythress. See Frame's "Primer on Perspectivalism," available at http://www.frame-poythress.org/frame_articles/PrimerOnPerspectivalism.htm (accessed February 1, 2011).

touching different parts of an elephant. One man holds an elephant's trunk and says it is a tree limb. A second man grasps the elephant's leg and describes it as a tree trunk. The third holds the elephant's tail and insists it is a snake. They each know truth according to their perspective. But the reality is that each man holds the same elephant. They lose sight of the whole truth, the absolute reality that an elephant is in the room. Naïve pluralism exists because people would rather have their personal hold on life than do the hard work of discovering the truth.

Basically, wherever naïve pluralism reigns, religious gullibility sits enthroned with it. Just when Western culture is becoming most uncritical, accepting, and open in pluralism, in comes Islam. Now, the irony is this: despite some brief historic periods of openness, Islam is not a liberal or pluralistic religion.

So what happens when a culture becomes naïvely pluralistic and encounters a religious system that is not? The culture welcomes the religious system with wide-open arms, and the religious system slowly works toward dominance. That's why it is important to ask our second set of questions.

2) What Is Islam, and Why Is It Not Consistently Compatible with Pluralism?

What Is Islam?

Islam is a religion, of course, but not primarily a theology. Islam is a religion with one major creed—the *shahada* or confession that "God is one and Muhammad is his messenger." This means that if we think of Islam in categories typical to Christian thought (systematic theology, for example), we will fundamentally misunderstand what Islam is. In one sense, given Islam's radical view of Allah's transcendence, his utter otherness, we might say the religion is largely agnostic. Because God is beyond finding out and knowing personally, the Muslim believes he cannot assert anything about the essence of God. Therefore, Islamic theology largely boils down to a series of negations—what God is *not*—rather than assertions about the essence of God.

Islam is not an institution but primarily an identity. When we think of being Christians, most of us retain as a primary identifier some other label or categorization. We think of ourselves as African-American Christians, Baptist Christians, and so on. Often those other identifiers come first. Islam reverses that. Of *first* importance is to be Muslim; the second thing is to belong to a national or ethnic category.

So Islam lays great stress on the brotherhood and solidarity of all Muslims and makes vastly secondary those considerations so often prominent in our thinking. From its earliest history of conquest and conversion, through the great Caliphates and empires, to the development of its law and tradition, there grew an intense solidarity, belonging, and identity as Muslim.

One Muslim writer states it well: "In the last analysis the solidarity engendered by Islam stems not from a rallying institution or figure, *but from pride of belonging.*"[5] Over a billion people practice Islam and regard themselves as Muslims on every continent of the earth. "But be he a Nigerian or a Pakistani, an Egyptian or an Iranian, his historical heritage still favors pride of identity inside the pale of Islam over pride of adherence to nationality."[6] This is why any perceived attack against Islam the religion gets regarded as an attack against Muslims everywhere. Recall the widespread protests when one European newspaper featured unflattering editorial cartoons of the prophet Muhammad. An outcry went up from Muslims all over the world. Why? To understand the Muslim response we must understand that Islam is primarily an identity. Muslims regard themselves as Muslims wherever they are.

Islam has religious pillars but is a system for governing all of life. Islam cannot be reduced to its five pillars or religious practices.[7] The pillars are no doubt important. But if we reduce Islam to these religious duties, we will fundamentally misunderstand what Islam is.

The major goal of Islam is to *Dar al-Islam*, to bring the "house of

---

[5]Cesar E. Farah, *Islam: Beliefs and Observances* (New York: Barron's, 2003), 10; emphasis added.
[6]Ibid, 14.
[7]The five pillars—*shahada*, prayer, alms, fasting, and pilgrimage—emerged as a consensus regarding the *religious* duties of the faith. Early in the history of Islam some Muslim clerics and scholars argued *jihad* should be the fifth pillar because *jihad*, or striving in the cause of Allah, runs throughout the entire practice of the faith. For a discussion, see Farah, *Islam*, 176.

Islam" or ruling precept and practice of Islam to every area of society. Islam seeks to regulate not just the religious life of the Muslim but *all* of life—economic, family, military, and so on.

Incidentally, as a convert from Islam, this is why I am very cautious and skeptical about contextualization approaches to Muslim evangelism that leaves the convert in the outward forms and practices of Islam. The forms are as integral to Islam as the theology. Islam is significantly constituted by outward form. If you take someone who converts from Islam and leave him in that outward form, my experience says you are not serving him as effectively as possible. As a convert, it took me years, for example, to remove the Qur'an from its exalted place in my home, because the system of Islam still had its strong tentacles on me. Converts need to be helped with the sucking, entangling system of Islamic forms, even if it means wisely facing persecution and other risks.

How is this goal of *Dar al-Islam* sought? It is not done by teaching the pillars of Islam but by advancing *sharia*, the law of Islam. So if we want to think about Islam more carefully, we must think about *sharia*.

What Is Sharia?

Sharia is basically the system of laws that govern Islamic life. One Muslim writer describes *sharia* as "the epitome of the true Islamic spirit, the most decisive expression of Islamic thought, the essential kernel of Islam."[8] Another Muslim writer says simply, "The Sharia is Islam's constitution."[9] For many Muslims and Muslim leaders, the *sharia* is the fullest embodiment of the Islamic ideal. *Sharia* is what we are contending with in our encounter with Islam—not prayer on Friday. We are contending with *sharia*, the whole of it, not a few practices and theological ideas abstracted from it.

From the beginning of the spread of Islam, the Islamic community needed more than just the "five pillars" to shape and govern life. In the prophet Muhammad's lifetime and the generations following, Islam entered into more and more lands—from Arabia, Africa,

---

[8]Ferah, *Islam*, 201
[9]Ibid., 160.

Europe, Asia, and beyond—with differing local cultures and sometimes differing approaches to authority in the community. As Islam spread, great empires were founded and established. With the spread of Islam, major questions developed: How do you regulate life under an Islamic ideal with such a diversity of people coming into Islam through conquest, conversion, and caravan trading? How are we going to govern this life? It was a pressing question of authority and coherence. This meant that a more uniform standard for governing life and society was needed. In the first two to three centuries of the Islamic empire, we find the development and codification of *sharia* to answer this need.

Four sources were combined to comprise *sharia*.[10] The obvious starting place was the Qur'an. Every Muslim believed that the Qur'an revealed God's will for man's life. In it were the signs or miracles from God, through the prophet, that were to be obeyed. During his lifetime, Muhammad served not only as the religious leader of Islam but also as civic leader, judge, and military general. After his lifetime, the companions and successors of Muhammad had to figure out how to govern the expanding empire under Islamic rule. Early in Islam's development, Muslim leaders recognized that effective application of the Qur'an required some commentary.

So, added to the Qur'an as a second source for *sharia* were the *sunna* and *hadith*. The *sunna* recorded the life and ways of Muhammad, while the *hadith* became a collection of sayings attributed to the prophet. The companions of the prophet and the wider Muslim community looked to these writings for guidance in Islamic society. Eventually, some Muslim scholars would come to regard the *sunna* and *hadith* with as much authority as the Qur'an itself. So today you will meet some Muslims who claim you cannot properly understand the Qur'an unless you speak Arabic and without consulting the *sunna* and *hadith*. So, *sharia* finds its basis not just in the precepts of the Qur'an but also in the example and sayings of the prophet Muhammad as perfect exemplar.

Third, religious belief and practices among orthodox Muslims

---

[10]For brief discussions of the development of Islamic law, see ibid., 159–65; and Albert Hourani, *A History of the Arab Peoples* (New York: Warner, 1991), 65–69, 113–16, 160–62.

could be established by the principle of analogy. Keep in mind we are not talking about a system of case law or systematized doctrine. So, whenever a situation arose not answered clearly by the Qur'an or *hadith*, the Islamic judge was permitted to find a situation from the Qur'an or *hadith* that was analogous in motive, cause, or material similarity and base a ruling on that information. One reason for this principle was the Islamic aversion to "innovation" and private interpretation, which were seen as weakening fidelity to the Qur'an and *hadith*. As analogies are added, there is pressure to codify quickly.

Finally, there was the consensus of the communities. Things not sanctioned specifically by the Qur'an, but nevertheless practiced by the Muslim faithful, could become legal through consensus and inclusion in *sharia*. How consensus was obtained varied from location to location. And as you might expect, the commonly accepted traditions and practices varied from context to context. But by the third century after the prophet's lifetime, there were traditions incorporated into *sharia*.

This is how *sharia* developed in the Islamic world. And it is under this rule that Muslims seek to live.

Three Challenges to the Islamic Ideal of Sharia

Over the last two hundred years, the advance of Islam has faced three significant challenges: the competing ideals and military might of the West, secularism, and internal weakness. In the face of these challenges, some Muslim groups look to *sharia* for recovery of Islamic strength and progress.

The *traditionalist* or fundamentalist says, "Purify Islam by advancing a pristine *sharia* and reforming society." We find this approach in the Wahabbism of Saudi Arabia and Sudan, in Libya, Qatar, UAE, and Iran since the revolution. But the *modernist* takes the opposite approach. He says, "No, we need to reform Islam and *sharia* while advancing society." This is the approach of Egypt, India, Syria, and Indonesia. Meanwhile, the smaller group of *secularists* seeks to divide Islam and secular society, as in modern-day Turkey. Most Muslims fall into either modernists or traditionalists groups, with the traditionalists often riding the coattails of the modernists.

So, we often see the modernist face of Islam, which appears compatible with good pluralistic ideals, but traditionalists follow in the modernist wake, and societies end up with *sharia* being advanced in some way.

Why Is Sharia Not Consistently Compatible with Pluralism?

There are four brief reasons *sharia* is not compatible with a healthy pluralism:

1) *Sharia,* at best, is theocratic and theonomistic at the very least. If *sharia* is the "constitution of Islam," then *sharia* offers very different legal footing from American constitutional law. American constitutional law is grounded in natural law and individual liberty when the Declaration of Independence declares, "We hold these truths to be self-evident, that all men are created equal, that they are endowed by their Creator with certain unalienable rights, that among these are life, liberty and the pursuit of happiness." But Islam declares that Allah rules all things, and all societies must be brought under the rule of Islam.

2) Because *sharia* leaves no room for modernization or flexibility in interpretation, it leaves no room for healthy pluralism. With the Islamic bias against "innovation" and "interpretation," s*haria* remains largely locked into the body of rulings and ideas set within the first three hundred years of the Muslim era (ninth century).

3) Because *sharia* incorporates cultural consensus into law, the certain cultural practices enter into the legal framework of countries unaware. In our context, when we refer to "cultural practices," we do not necessarily associate such things with a particular *religious* practice. So a person may participate in a cultural milieu without our necessarily making any religious assumptions about that practice at all. But in Islam, culture is religion and religion is culture. So to admit elements of *sharia* into the legal framework of any country such as the United States under the guise of "cultural practice" or "multiculturalism" is to give ground to *sharia* and to establish a constitutional footing quite at odds with the assumptions the country was founded upon. We cannot admit cultural practices into Western law without

opening the gate to all of *sharia*. Think, for example, about Muslim women in France wearing veils, until recently, while driving. Most people think of the veil largely as a cultural preference or practice issue. But the adorning of veils is as much about *sharia* and its legal requirements as it is about culture. Protecting the wearing of veils begins the process of extending other *sharia*-inspired practices in Western societies.

4) Advocacy for *sharia* sometimes reaches a point where it can no longer tolerate difference or accept minority status. If Muslim communities come to define *sharia* as the only acceptable framework for living freely and worshiping freely as Muslims, then we can understand why substantial Muslim minorities in places like the Philippines and Indonesia look to secede from the wider country to form separate Muslim states. And if living under *sharia* becomes the only acceptable way to live, we understand why militarism and force become acceptable strategies for some people. Such Muslims view aggressive advocacy and militarism as self-defense or acceptable *jihad* because their view of *sharia* does not include Western-styled pluralism.

3) What Should the Christian Response Be to Islam?

The Christian lives in two kingdoms or cities. The Christian is both a citizen of a nation and a citizen of heaven. Therefore, our response must distinguish between these two kingdoms and our responsibility in each.

How Should We Respond to Islam?

When I am asked, "How should we respond to Islam?" I am usually being asked a political question. The questioner usually wants to know how to act as a citizen of the United States in response to the growth of Islam. They ask a policy-level question.

Here is what I would say: as a citizen of the United States, work for the faithful continuance and application of the nonestablishment and free exercise clause. Constitutionally, Congress shall not make any laws that establish religion or prohibit the free exercise thereof.

Now, that is a bit of constitutional genius. Granted, it is not always well applied. But it needs to be—especially in our engagement with Islam. What the nonestablishment clause prohibits is the adoption of laws that make a religion something the state supports. This means that at least in the American constitutional system *sharia* and elements of *sharia* are off-limits. The main way to hold back the inappropriate advance of Islamic law and custom—which tend to restrict basic liberties—is to consistently apply the nonestablishment clause.

But, at the same time, Congress cannot make any laws that prohibit the free exercise of religion. Here, we want to defend our Muslim neighbor's rights to worship according to the dictates of his own conscience and not be afraid to do so. As citizens of an earthly kingdom, we want to be hospitable, kind, and diligent in pursuing that fundamental liberty called "religious freedom." We want to work for such freedom so we can honestly and faithfully engage our Muslim neighbors with the gospel. This is how we maintain a good pluralism—we resist the establishment of religion while promoting free exercise.

How Should We Respond to Muslims?

But sometimes I am asked the question, "How should I respond or talk to my Muslim neighbor or friend?" That is a street-level question that's really about our citizenship in heaven. Here, I would counsel a few things drawn from Matthew 10.

First, remember the gospel. "As you go, preach this message: 'The kingdom of heaven is near'" (Matt. 10:7 NIV). As citizens of the kingdom of heaven, our main responsibility is to proclaim this message, to make Jesus known, to be ambassadors of Christ. We are to speak of his love, grace, judgment, coming, and salvation.

However, I fear many of us lack confidence in the gospel. When I am asked, "How do I witness to my Muslim friend?" most people want me to tell them something other than the gospel. They want a trick or a secret. They are asking, "What worked for you? Can I push that same 'easy' button?" But the button was the gospel! The secret was Christ and him crucified, buried, and resurrected to save sinners from the wrath of a holy God, to make them new creatures, and bring them into the family of God!

When our mouths are open and the gospel comes out, divine power comes out. The Word gives life and makes people new. Think about how powerful our speaking is. Apart from God, we are the only speaking beings in existence. And the form of speaking that has the most power is the gospel. Be confident in the gospel and talk about Jesus. That same gospel that saved you and me is the same gospel that will save our Muslim neighbors and friends.

Let us have confidence in this gospel. The gospel is the power of God unto salvation. Have confidence in the gospel. God puts power—saving power—in our mouths. So as the gospel goes out, the Spirit grants life. Have confidence in that. Trust it. Share it.

Second, return to the world. Jesus says, "I am sending you out like sheep among wolves. Therefore be as shrewd as snakes and as innocent as doves" (Matt. 10:16 NIV). Here is a verse that calls the Christian to be a thinker. It calls us to face devouring wolves with intelligence and purity. There are a lot of animals in this verse, but it is no petting zoo. The world is a dangerous place, and Jesus sends his people into it.

But do not think that because Jesus sends his people into the world as sheep for slaughter, that he wastes our lives. He does not! The Father does not waste the lives of those he has purchased with the blood of his Son. So Jesus says to go into the world with the gospel and know that you need to be wise and pure because a dangerous world opposes you. We will face persecution (vv. 17–20), betrayal (vv. 21–23), and slander (vv. 24–25). I don't know anyone who knows this truth as personally and painfully as men and women from Muslim backgrounds.

Once during a visit to the Middle East, someone introduced me to a young man from Saudi Arabia. He came to faith in Christ while attending university in the United States. After his conversion, he returned home during the Christmas break and took with him his Bible and some Christian music hidden in his bag. While at home, his mother went through his things, found his Bible and music, and, along with the men of his family, confronted him. They demanded to know if he had converted to Christianity and if he had been baptized. Under serious threat, he confessed he had converted but had not yet been baptized. The family immediately forced him to recant, withdrew him from his studies, and kept him under house arrest for two years. When I met him, he had finally been allowed to move to another country in the region to continue studies.

The thought of ever renouncing Jesus still grieved him bitterly. He wanted to speak with me about his plans to be baptized and to return home to profess his faith to his family. He feared being disowned at the least, and possibly more. He knew what he would face, but he also knew Jesus sent him into the world bearing testimony of his glory, grace, and love.

Jesus sends us out to engage the world. So it is no surprise that lands once Christian but that adopted monasticism and withdrawal from the culture are now thoroughly Muslim. They failed to go out!

Third, repent of fear. "Do not be afraid of those who kill the body but cannot kill the soul. Rather, be afraid of the One who can destroy both soul and body in hell" (Matt. 10:28 NIV). The one who has all authority in heaven and earth and promises to be with us always says, "Do not be afraid." That fear is destroying our love for our neighbors, destroying evangelistic and missionary zeal, and destroying souls.

Recently I had the privilege of participating in a radio interview to discuss the topic of witnessing to Muslims. While on the program, the host told me of a caller who said of Muslim evangelism, "Let them stay over there. They don't want to hear the gospel or want us in their lands, so let them stay over there. Let them perish in their sins." Where is the weeping over hell? In our fear, we betray the fact that we may not have begun to weep over the reality of 1.5 billion people made in God's image perishing in everlasting torment and judgment. This man did not know what spirit he was of.

We must repent of fear. And instead, think on God's providence and provision (Matt. 10:29–31). His eye is on the sparrow; we know he watches us. Not one passage of Scripture gives us the slightest grounds for fear!

Fourth, retrieve the reward. "Whoever finds his life will lose it, and whoever loses his life for my sake will find it. . . . If anyone gives even a cup of cold water to one of these little ones because he is my disciple, I tell you the truth, he will certainly not lose his reward" (Matt. 10:39, 42 NIV). Christian, throw safety and security and ease and comfort and convenience to the dogs! Give yourself to something greater—the glory of God and the joy of God. Jesus is our reward. Lose your life for Jesus and the gospel so that you will find your life. Give that cup of water—in other words, do even small acts of mercy in the name of Jesus and the gospel—and you will have a reward you cannot lose. Count it all loss so that you might gain Christ. Stop fearing man—and go get your reward, which is loving fellowship with God in heaven. God is your portion, your inheritance. And to everyone who goes out with the gospel of the kingdom, God gives himself as the fulfillment of all their hopes and joy. Go get him.

Can you imagine that day? Psalm 17:15 says when we awake in our righteousness, we shall see him and be satisfied. That is what lies on the other side of the Christian's engagement with Islam—satisfaction, joy unspeakable and full of glory. Don't you want it? Let's go get it.

*   *   *

Father,
Make these words helpful and useful for our souls. Stir up your people. Lord, most of the readers of this chapter, if not all, know the gospel, so they know everything they need, to see Muslims come to know you.

Grant us confidence that comes from resting in your power. Grant us boldness that comes from resting in your grace and not in our thoughts and intellects. Grant us boldness to open our mouths and speak as we ought.

May Muslim people, made in your image, made for your glory, intended to be around your throne, hear this good news and be saved for the glory of your name and the joy of the nations.

In Jesus's name we pray.
Amen

5

Think Hard, Stay Humble:
The Life of the Mind and the Peril of Pride

FRANCIS CHAN

> Now concerning food offered to idols: we know that "all of us possess knowledge." This "knowledge" puffs up, but love builds up. If anyone imagines that he knows something, he does not yet know as he ought to know. But if anyone loves God, he is known by God.
>
> 1 CORINTHIANS 8:1–3

I don't know if there is a more appropriate passage for us to turn to at this point in the book than 1 Corinthians 8:1–3. It is a passage directed toward those whose have their facts right but hearts wrong. Here Paul addresses the intelligent but unloving.

It has been wonderful and challenging for me to study this passage. Meditating on 1 Corinthians 8:1–3 caused me to realize how many statements I make each day that are not motivated by love. It has caused me to pray that God would remind me to love each person I encounter and to seek to build up each individual with my words.

Do I Genuinely Love?

Years ago, a friend of mine asked me how I prepared to preach. I told him how I pictured God in the room and that I would tell him that

I wanted to please him alone. I then asked my friend how he would prepare. He told me how he would look at the crowd and pray, "God, you know how I love these people. Give me the right words to bring them closer to you." He then explained that there are other times that he would have to pray, "Father, I don't love these people like I should. Give me a greater love for them." It is sad that I had been preaching for years, I realized then, without thinking about really loving the people to whom I preached.

Now I keep a list of questions in the front of my Bible. It is a checklist that I try to run through each time before I speak. I am "prone to wander," as the old hymn says. My motives for preaching can be very unholy at times. These seven questions can be good checks on my sinful heart. The first two questions are especially relevant to the theme of this chapter:

1) Am I concerned with what others will think of my message or what God will think?
2) Do I genuinely love these people?

When my heart is right, preaching becomes a wonderful experience rather than a burdensome one.[1]

Worried about Whose Presence?

The first time I spoke at my college alma mater, I was an absolute wreck. The president of our college, John MacArthur, was sitting in the front row. Every time I told a joke, I would look out of the corner of my eye to see if he was laughing. Whenever I made a point, I would check to see if I had his approval. It was not a good experience.

What made it worse was, when I was done, my wife asked me, "What was that all about? You definitely were not yourself up there."

My response was, "But John MacArthur was in the front row."

To which Lisa replied, "Let me get this straight. You were preach-

---

[1] The full list of seven questions I rehearse before speaking is as follows: (1) Am I worried about what people think of my message or what God thinks? (Teach with fear.) (2) Do I genuinely love these people? (Teach with love.) (3) Am I accurately presenting this passage? (Teach with accuracy.) (4) Am I depending on the Holy Spirit's power or my own cleverness? (Teach with power.) (5) Have I applied this message to my own life? (Teach with integrity.) (6) Will this message draw attention to me or to God? (Teach with humility.) (7) Do the people really need this message? (Teach with urgency.)

ing Psalm 139, speaking about the presence of God. Yet you were worried about the presence of John MacArthur?"

Foolishly defending myself, I began to explain to my wife all of Dr. MacArthur's accomplishments. I hoped at least to help her see why I would be afraid. Her response was, "And all of his righteous deeds are as filthy rags." Ouch.

Written in Love

I have come a long way since those days, but I would be lying if I told you I hadn't given any thought to the fact that I was going to be preaching to some of my heroes when I delivered the original version of this chapter at the 2010 Desiring God National Conference in Minneapolis.

Yet, by the grace of God, I think I was able to look beyond all of that and think more about loving them. I asked God to help me use whatever giftedness I have for their benefit and edification. He gave me love for them. And now I ask him for that love for you, the reader. This chapter is written in love. I have been praying for you, that you would love God and others more as a result of this study of 1 Corinthians 8.

What Matters in Eternity

Think about this: those of us who are in Christ will be together one hundred years from now. I've tried to write this chapter in light of that—thinking that I will see your face one hundred years from now. And two hundred years from now. With that perspective, I ask, "What can I write to you in this chapter that will matter in eternity?" *Oh, God, help me love these readers.*

This passage in 1 Corinthians 8:1–3 is so fitting for this book because it addresses people that technically have the right theology but are wrong because of their lack of love. As I've studied this passage, the Lord has taught me so much. But the main thing he did was give me love for you. I hope, as you read this chapter, that you see me as your brother in Christ now and into eternity and see that God wants us to have love for one another.

Meat Offered to Idols

The issue in 1 Corinthians 8 that Paul addresses is meat offered to idols. The Corinthians had come out of pagan backgrounds. They once had worshiped idols. They had believed that meat was inhabited by demons, so they would offer the meat before their idol. The idea was that the idol would cleanse the meat of the demons, so when they consumed the meat, it would be clean and inhabited by their god rather than by demons. It was an act of worship to their idol. They had grown up doing it this way—and some of them were still affected by this way of thinking.

But some of the Corinthian believers who were more knowledge-able were saying, "Idols aren't real. Now that we're Christians, we know that idols are a farce. Just eat the meat. It's not a big deal." But the weaker Christians who had spent their whole lives thinking another way, having not yet reached a certain Christian maturity in thinking, were sensing in their consciences, *I can't eat that meat. It's been offered to an idol. That's like worshiping an idol, and I can't eat it.* Meanwhile the more knowledgeable Christians were saying, "Just eat it. There's no such thing as an idol." So listening to this informed but unloving counsel, the consciences of the less knowledgeable were being wounded.

So Paul addresses the problem. "Yes, you're right; the idols are not really gods. But that's not the point. The point is that in using your knowledge, you weren't thinking about your brother. He didn't yet feel right in his conscience about taking the meat, and yet you unlovingly pushed him toward it because of your knowledge. You wounded his conscience. Why would you do that?" *Why in the world would you do that to your brother?*

Look what Paul says in verse 13: "If food makes my brother stumble, I will never eat meat, lest I make my brother stumble." Paul loves his brothers and sisters in Christ so much that if he knew that their seeing him eat meat would cause them to stumble, then he simply will stop eating meat. He'll go vegan. Eating meat is not that big of a deal compared to loving his brother. He loves his brother more than his freedom to eat meat. So, these more knowledgeable Christians are right that it is okay to eat meat, but their problem is that they are not thinking for their less knowledgeable brothers.

In verse 11, Paul says, "And so by your knowledge this weak person is destroyed, *the brother for whom Christ died*." With your knowledge, you are hurting your brother for whom Christ died. Wow. And if that's not enough, he says in verse 12, "Thus, sinning against your brothers and wounding their conscience when it is weak, you sin against Christ." Such unloving use of knowledge against a fellow Christian amounts to sin against Jesus himself!

Paul grants that, technically, the stronger, more knowledgeable brothers are right, at least about the meat offered to idols. But their hearts are wrong. "Yes, yes, idols are not real. But look what you did! You got your brother whose conscience wouldn't allow him to eat that meat to eat it anyway." The stronger ate of it themselves and said to their weaker brothers, "Come on, just eat. It's not that big of a deal." Yet Paul says that if he could hurt a brother that way, then he would be eager to never eat meat again. Because he loved them so much. "That's my brother for whom Christ died. I love him."

Paul's Admirable Love

I admire this so much about Paul. We all admire his theology and his understanding of God. But what I admire equally about Paul, perhaps even more, is his love for people. Don't you see it in his writings? He has a passion for people—whoever he's around.

Maybe his most shocking statement about love for others is Romans 9:1–3, which surprises me every time I read it. There he says:

> I'm speaking the truth in Christ—I am not lying; my conscience bears me witness in the Holy Spirit—that I have great sorrow and unceasing anguish in my heart. For I could wish that I myself were accursed and cut off from Christ for the sake of my brothers, my kinsmen according to the flesh.

I have studied these verses over and over again, because my initial response was to think, *That's impossible!* I think I love people, but I can't imagine making a statement like Paul's. "I . . . wish that I myself were accursed and cut off from Christ for the sake of my brothers." *That must be hyperbole*, I think. It's one thing to love people, but the thought of being willing to be cut off from Christ for their sake? Have you loved like that before? I don't know if I could do that for anyone. And since Paul expects that people like me will think he is exaggerating, he starts the passage with, "I am speaking the truth in Christ—I am not lying; my conscience bears me witness in the Holy Spirit." He is not exaggerating. He hurts that badly. He means these words. He has "great sorrow and unceasing anguish" in his heart.

Does that describe you? Do you have great sorrow and unceasing anguish in your heart for those who don't know Jesus?

Unceasing anguish.

When we look at Paul's life and see how he went from place to place trying to win people to Jesus by telling them the good news, and we see all the persecutions he was willing to endure, then his life really does make sense of this passage. Look at his life, and it becomes clear that he believed this. If Rick Warren is right in chapter 1 that we only really believe those doctrines that we actually live out, then we see in Paul's life that he really did have great sorrow and unceasing anguish for the lost. He had such love, it seems, that he really could wish that he were accursed and cut off from Christ for the sake of his unbelieving friends and family.

Thinking about People

Many of you reading this chapter, no doubt, are very good thinkers. The thinking part of this book is exciting for you. You love it, and you cheer it on because you think very hard, hopefully through the Scriptures. My challenge to you in this chapter is this: *How hard do you think about people? How hard do you think about loving your fellow Christians? And how hard do you think about the lost?*

The Intrigue of Christian Love

Thabiti Anyabwile says in chapter 4 that if we truly care for Muslims, then we will reach out to them with the love of Christ. I sat next to a Muslim one time on a plane on my way to Africa. Eventually I asked him about his beliefs, and then he asked me about mine. When I told him how Jesus changed my life, he said, "I hope you're not one of those radicals." He said he used to wait tables and have Christians preach at him. I didn't respond directly at first. But I was praying. You can think about two things at once. While I was listening to him, I also was praying, *God, help me on this one. What in the world do I say? How do I love this man?* I had shared my testimony, but he obviously was so turned off by Christians that I didn't know where to go next.

A few minutes later as we were talking about other things, he asked, "Why are you going to Africa?"

"I went there a few years ago," I said, "and I saw these kids who had nothing. I saw them digging through trash heaps looking for water, for food, for anything. There's no education. They're just dwindling away." I told him that it broke my heart to see such poverty and that when I had returned home, I started selling what I could and getting my friends to do the same. Then our church started giving more and more, and we began building schools for them and teaching them how to farm. "I'm going back to see some of that. I'm so excited."

He just looked at me. His eyes got big, and he said, "That is amazing to me." And here's what was so fascinating. He then said, "I prayed that I would meet someone like you. I've never understood the charity of some Christians—why they would sacrifice their own stuff for someone that they might not even know. Tell me more about this."

Suddenly he was interested.

I said, "We see in Scripture that we're to become more and more like Jesus, who had it all but didn't consider equality with God something to be grasped, so he emptied himself. As his followers, we're to do the same. He laid down his life for us, and we should lay down our lives for others. That's why we do what we do."

What changed everything for this man was hearing that we loved. Something intrigued him about these Christians that he was otherwise disgusted with, these "radical" Christians—and that something was our love.

Weeping for the Lost

When is the last time you wept for the lost?

When I became a Christian in high school, I started looking

differently at all my friends who didn't know Jesus. It consumed me—that grief, that sorrow, that *unceasing anguish* that Paul talks about. It was in me. I would cut class to tell people about Jesus. *This is bigger.*

I remember getting in my high school yearbook as a junior and thinking, "I may never again see these seniors that are graduating in a couple of weeks." I got on the phone and started calling everyone I knew. I said, "This is going to be the weirdest phone call you've ever received. We only barely know each other, and we may never hear from each other again, but I want to tell you about something that changed my life."

I started a Bible study on campus, thinking I was going to reach my whole school. *These are my friends. I love these guys. I want them saved.*

Feeling Unceasing Anguish

I remember waiting tables at a restaurant. You get so close to the other waiters and waitresses. It's like a little clique. You get together and complain about your customers or the managers. It's quite the bond.

The other waiters would go out together to get drunk and take me along to drive them home. I remember sharing Jesus with them. And I remember one day having so much fun with them at Six Flags and coming home and weeping and begging God: "God, you can't let these people go to hell. I love them, Lord. I love them. Do something, please. I know I can't do anything for them ultimately. But you say that the prayer of a righteous man is powerful and effective, and so I want all the sin out of my life. I want to be as righteous as I can. I want you to hear me and save these people." I've felt some of this unceasing anguish.

Anguish at My Grandmother's Death

I will never forget the death of my grandmother. It was the most painful moment in my life. She had come to the United States from Hong Kong and had raised me for part of my life. I loved her, and she didn't believe in Jesus. She had a stroke, and the doctors waited for me to get there before turning off the machine. She was brain dead, they said, and there we were—just me, my brother, and my grand-mother—in the hospital room. I got down by the bed and screamed in her ear in Chinese, trying to explain the gospel. I cried out, "God, I know you can't just save her apart from faith in your Son. You can't just let her into heaven without Jesus. They say she's brain dead, but you can change that. Can you just get her to hear my voice? That's all I'm asking. Just let me share some of the things I never got to share."

I was crying like a baby, grabbing her hand, saying, "Grandma, please believe. You know you were wrong. I'm telling you Jesus is the way to heaven. You must have him." As I shared I was hoping that maybe she would open an eye or give me some sort of sign. Maybe she would squeeze my hand and show me that she heard the message.

But there was nothing.

I saw the EKG monitor bottoming out. I thought I was going to go nuts. It was the one time in my life that I wanted to take the Bible and just toss it—because since I believe this Book, I knew my grand-mother was going to suffer beginning right then. It's been twenty years since, and has she been suffering that whole time? Are you kidding me? I want to erase these things. I don't want to think hard about the truth of the wrath of God. I don't want to think hard about people like that.

But this kind of thinking, with its accompanying pain, motivates us. And it motivated Paul. He had unceasing anguish over the lost, and he had to do something about it.

How Much Do You Love?

As my grandmother was dying, my brother was in the room, and at the time he was not walking with Jesus. I looked at my brother and said, "Listen, Paul. I don't ever want to see you like this. I don't ever want to see you in a hospital room and wonder where you're going. You have to change your life. Give your life to Jesus. Not just praying a little prayer. I mean, *follow him*—seriously follow him. You need to turn."

My brother said that he had thought he believed, until he saw me talking to Grandma that day. That's when he realized that he didn't: "I don't believe like you believe." So he looked at me and said, "Okay, okay. I'll change, I'll change." At the time, I thought he was just saying it, but sure enough, a few weeks later he would say, "Francis, literally everything has changed. I've changed. I'm going to marry the girl I'm with. No more drinking, no partying, no nothing. I'm even driving the speed limit." (Wow, I thought, you didn't have to go *that* far!)

A couple of years later he said, "Francis, I think God is calling me to be a pastor. I want to go to seminary." Now he is a pastor working with the homeless in San Francisco. It is everything I prayed for— my big brother to whom I was scared to talk about Jesus is walking with Jesus! But at that moment, when Grandma was dying, I wasn't intimidated. Only one thing was on my mind: my unceasing anguish for my brother.

That unceasing anguish motivates us to talk. And it is love that produces such anguish. So I ask the question, *How much do you love?*

Loving until We Started Learning

I remember the time the elders at our church began confessing how we once loved people more. We once hurt more for the poor. We once loved the lost more. And then we started learning.

Years before, someone had told me that my theology wasn't quite right and that I should step out of the church environment and learn some things first. I started learning, doing Bible study after Bible study, and realizing how much I didn't know. So I thought I should go to Bible college. One class at a time, I was getting further and further away from unbelievers.

At Bible college, I realized how I really didn't know much, and so I went to seminary. There I realized even more that I didn't know much! I kept going down this trail where I thought, "I have to know more, I have to know more." That eagerness to learn can be good. But the problem comes when we leave this world of lost people to a greater and greater degree. We become increasingly secluded. We might think hard about the Scriptures, but we are no longer thinking about people—at least about lost people, if not about our fellow believers as well.

Yet somehow the apostles were able to do both. They grew in their knowledge of God, *and* they grew in their love for people. Their unceasing anguish never stopped. They kept pursuing knowledge *and* people, thinking about the Scriptures *and* thinking about the lost.

Is that true of you? As you are learning, are you still loving? As you acquire more knowledge, are you still burdened like you once were? Does it break your heart right now that you have brothers and sisters in Christ around the world who will never have a book like this and benefit from teaching like this? Maybe they are just trying to find water right now so that they can survive. What does that do to you?

There are mothers who don't have a clue about the stuff we casually debate in our classrooms but know they have kids that need to be fed today somehow. What does it do for you to think about the abducted little girls in Thailand who are being raped repeatedly as you read these pages? Does it do anything? Is there love?

Knowledge in the Service of Love

I love what Al Mohler says in chapter 2 about caring for the younger generation, and the way they think, and how we need to think hard so we can help them change their mind-set. I am worried about this generation and their eternal destiny. If they keep thinking with that type of worldview, then they are not headed to eternity with God. Does that break your heart? Does that motivate you?

Why do you learn? Do you learn because you love? Because you love so much and you think I want to help somehow? Do you think, "I love these people and want to help them somehow, and the only way is if I can understand this stuff"?

Others Seeing God in Our Love

First John 4:12 says, "No one has ever seen God; if we love one another, God abides in us and his love is perfected in us." Here the apostle John is talking about the love that we Christians should have for one another. When you look at your Christian brothers and sisters, do you honestly love them? Do you say, "That's my brother—if he were ever in trouble, I would be right there with him"?

Is that the type of love you have for those around you? God means that we embody this kind of love. When John writes, "No one has ever seen God," do you get it? Here's what he's saying: if we could love each other the way God loves us, then someone who doesn't even know God, someone who's never seen his beauty spiritually, may be able to see the love of God in our love for each other. Just as Jesus embodied God in the incarnation as God in the flesh, so there is a sense in which this is passed on to us. In our love for others, we now incarnate God's love, so to speak, because others see the love of God in us in a way they would not otherwise. As people come into our gatherings, do they see so much love that they actually get a glimpse of God? Or do they only see a lot of knowledge on display?

Knowledge with an Attitude

In 1 Corinthians 8:1, after Paul turns our attention to the topic of "food offered to idols," he says that "we know that 'all of us possess knowledge.'" "All of us possess knowledge" is a quotation. It's a phrase that the Corinthians were using to talk about what they assumed everyone knew. Now, Paul is not against us possessing knowledge. He is not saying, "Don't think," or even, "Don't think hard." But he is talking about the attitude behind the knowledge.

I was playing on the playground as an eight-year-old when I first heard the phrase, "No, duh!" I said something, then this girl looked at me and said, "No, duh!" I remember thinking, "What does that mean?" Behind it was an attitude. "Come on. Everyone knows it." And that's the attitude here of these Corinthians with so much knowledge. They are saying, "You know what? We all know. We all possess this knowledge." It had an attitude: "Come on. Everyone knows there's no such thing as idols." Paul says that this kind of knowledge puffs up. It's all about you. It's cold and stale and all about *you* having the knowledge. He explains in verses 4–6:

Therefore, as to the eating of food offered to idols, we know that "an idol has no real existence," and that "there is no God but one." For although there may be so-called gods in heaven or on earth—as indeed there are many "gods" and many "lords"—yet for us there is one God, the Father, from whom are all things and for whom we exist, and one Lord, Jesus Christ, through whom are all things and through whom we exist.

In other words, Paul says, "An idol doesn't have any real existence. We know that. You're right." But then in verse 7 he says, "However, not all possess this knowledge. But some, through former association with idols, eat food as really offered to an idol, and their conscience, being weak, is defiled." He says some of the Corinthian believers have this knowledge, but not all of them do. Some aren't ready yet for the application of such knowledge. And the "stronger," more knowledgeable believers need to be mindful of where their "weaker" brothers are and not have this attitude toward them: "Well, we all know that." This type of knowledge puffs up. But love builds up.

Knowledge: Essential but Not Sufficient

Knowledge is essential, but it's not sufficient. It takes knowledge about this passage for me to write this chapter. We do need knowledge. That is at the heart of this book. We need to think. We must know the truth. Knowledge is essential.

But knowledge alone is not sufficient for the Christian life. It's not enough just to have knowledge. That's why Paul says in 1 Corinthians 13:2: "If I have prophetic powers, and understand all mysteries and all knowledge, and if I have all faith, so as to remove mountains, but have not love, I am nothing." It doesn't matter if I have all knowledge. Knowledge is important, yes. It's essential. We need it. *Think hard.* But it's not enough. Paul says even if he had all knowledge but didn't love, he would amount to nothing. In other words, you can be brilliant and worthless.

It would be like a great basketball player who never misses a shot but keeps shooting into the opponent's basket. He may say, "I was five for five today from the three-point line," but his teammates would respond, "But you're killing our team! You're shooting at the wrong basket!" He answers confidently, "But I did not miss." That is the kind of attitude that Paul is confronting here. *You might be brilliant, but you're killing our team. You're not building up the brothers; you're making them feel dumb and wounding their conscience. You're not stirring them up to love and good deeds. You just keep making them feel inadequate. By your knowledge, this weaker brother is being destroyed!*

Your brilliance is worthless if you're not building up your brother—and even worse if you're destroying him with your knowledge. So when you look at people, do you love them? Do you think, *Let me use my knowledge to build this person up?*

What Christians Say to Each Other

So often when I read statements on blogs (or tweets)—comments that brothers will write to those who are supposed to be fellow brothers—I think, "Where is the love?" It burdens me. I can't believe some of the things Christians say to each other in person—and maybe especially online (when you don't have to look them in the face). How is what you're saying supposed to build that brother—or anyone else who hears it or reads it? Our knowledge should be pressed into the service of love. It should serve to build each other up. That's what love does. It builds up. It looks to help others, not hurt them.

Thinking about Others

First Corinthians 13:2 makes me think about one of my heroes, Joni Eareckson Tada. She has been a quadriplegic for over forty years now. She started an amazing ministry that gets wheelchairs all around the world. The last time I was speaking with her, it became clear to me that she was hurting. There's so much pain. I didn't realize that, as a quadriplegic, she could feel so much pain. As we were talking, she grimaced and called to her assistant, and she said to me, "I'm sorry, Francis. I have to go. I'm just in so much pain right now."

Then recently she found out that she has cancer. So many of us have been hurting for her. She started her chemo treatments, and they were wiping her out. Then we found out she had pneumonia. It made me think, "Wow, here's the sweetest woman on the earth with forty years as a quadriplegic in this insurmountable pain. And then she has cancer, and then she's in chemo, and then she's struck with pneumonia. And while she has pneumonia she types me a letter encouraging me to stay strong!" *Francis, I love you as a brother. You stay strong in the faith. I believe in what you're doing.*

How can she be thinking about anyone else? When I have the flu, I'm only thinking of me. Love produces this kind of constant thinking about others. Which is essentially what humility is.

Love and Humility

Humility is not self-degradation. Putting yourself down is all about self. Humility is about thinking of others—considering others more important than yourself. Like Joni. In the midst of her pain and sickness, she thought, *I should encourage Francis. I wonder how he's doing.*

When I read her note, I cried, "O God, make me like this!" I want to be thinking constantly, *How can I build people up?* I want to think how I can encourage others to keep fighting for the King and his kingdom. How I can keep others focused on eternity? When my brother and sister are discouraged, how can I build them up? That's what love does. It builds people up.

In fact, Paul explains to the Corinthians who were using their gifts—gifts of knowledge, gifts of tongues, and more—to puff themselves up, that in doing so, they were thinking only about themselves and building themselves up. He explains to them in 1 Corinthians 12:7, "To each is given the manifestation of the Spirit *for the common good.*" Why did God gift you the way that he did? It's not for you alone. It's for all of us. In love and humility, we should be thinking constantly, *How can I build up the people around me?*

Paul writes, "'Knowledge' puffs up, but love builds up" (1 Cor. 8:1), and immediately after he adds, "If anyone imagines that he knows something, he does not yet know as he ought to know" (v. 2). These Christians, who were seemingly so knowledgeable, didn't really know as they should have known. In God's eyes, they were technically right on this issue, but they were only imagining themselves to be such knowledgeable, brilliant people. In God's eyes, it was not real knowledge. They were delusional. Because if they really knew, they would know that knowledge is meant to be used in the service of love. That's true knowledge in God's eyes. Such a person really gets it, is one who really *knows*.

True Knowledge

It is such a danger to puff yourself up and imagine that you're a brilliant person. It's like the school bully who imagines himself as the hero because he is the strongest. He can beat anyone up. But everyone else knows that he's not a hero but a jerk. If he were a real hero, he would defend the weak. He would be lifting them up, using his strength to care for them and protect them, not to bully them.

In the same way, with biblical and theological "knowledge" come the intellectual bullies who seem to know so much and imagine themselves to be so knowledgeable. But Paul is saying that they may be only imagining that they are knowledgeable, because if they really knew, they would use their knowledge not to weaken others but to strengthen them. Not to tear people down but to build them up. That's what love does.

Known by God

Paul says in verse 3, "But if anyone loves God, he is known by God." The point here is the power of love. Note that Paul doesn't say that if you know a bunch of information about God, then you are known by God. It has to do with *love* rather than with knowledge. In verse 3, if you *love* God, Paul says, then you are known by him. It's not about information. But when love is attached to knowledge, then it actually creates something—a relationship.

When you love God—when you don't only know all these facts about him, you don't merely understand some truths about him, but you actually love him—that's what signals this relationship with him. It's about the relationship.

Likewise in Galatians 4:9 Paul says, "Now that you have come to know God"—and here he breaks his train of thought—"or rather to be known by God . . . " I love that: not merely knowing but being "known by God." That's a huge difference. I had spent so much of my life thinking about my knowing God that I was blown away the first time I read this verse. "Known by God"—what a beautiful thought! I am known by God. He knows me.

It would be one thing for me to tell you I know someone world-famous, but it is quite another when that famous person mentions my name and thanks me at his next internationally televised press conference. It's not merely that I know him. *He knows me.* It makes all the difference in the world.

And wonder of all wonders, Paul says that we are "known by God." Why did Paul switch from *knowing* God to *being known* by him? He says in essence, "You know God—actually, here's a better way to say it: *You're known by him!*" God knows me. This is so personally significant.

Think about this: right now in heaven, on the throne of the universe, sits the most valuable and glorious Being possible. He is sovereign. He is in control of everything—including the last breath you took. Your breathing, and everything else going on in the universe, is fully in his hands. The angels are covering themselves and calling out, "Holy, Holy, Holy!" He dwells in inapproachable light. Yet if somehow you could go before God right now, physically, and ask him, "God Almighty, do you know me?" how amazing is it that he would look down right now on me writing this chapter, and on you reading it, and say, "I know you, and I love you. You are my child. I love *you*. I know *you*." The creator and sustainer of everything, the all-powerful one, knows you personally, and right now in heaven, because of his beloved Son, he sees you as his beloved child. Despite all the junk that is in our lives, he sent his Son to cover all of it. Now he looks at us and knows us and loves us. And he hears our prayers.

The God Who Hears Our Prayers

So, when I talk to God, I tell him the desires of my heart. I tell him how I want to bring glory to his name—what things I hope for in ministry. And I've seen amazing answers to these prayers. It is so incredible that I, little Francis Chan, can talk to God and he answers me! I can say, "God, here's what I'm thinking . . . ," and I'll see supernatural, amazing, unbelievable things happen. It blows my mind every time, because it reminds me that *I'm talking to God!* He hears me. He knows me. He listens to me. Whether it's silly little things or massive things. For hours I could tell you story after story about how God listens and answers—and so many times over such seemingly dumb things. He cares about both the little things and the huge things.

One time I was golfing with some friends. I'm not a great golfer, but I can hit the ball a long way. However, my friends had these big, expensive drivers, so they outdrove me. I felt discouraged and prayed, "God, I want one of those clubs." I was thinking I might eventually buy one or maybe ask for one for Christmas. But then I thought, *No, that's stupid. It's just ego and a waste of money.* So I thought, *No, Lord, I'm not going to waste the money like that.*

The next morning I went to speak at a conference at a little church plant, and when I was done speaking, the pastor said, "I hear that when you go to little churches, sometimes they'll give you an honorarium and you just hand it right back. So we didn't get you an honorarium. We bought you this driver." The whole way home in the car, I laughed and said, "Come on, Lord. Even a driver? Such a little thing as a driver?"

There have been so many times that Lisa and I, with tears rolling down our faces in amazement after he has so tangibly blessed us, will say, "Can we ever give to God without him, every single time, blessing us in return and blowing our minds by answering so many, and such seemingly insignificant, prayers?"

Answered Prayer on the Way Home from Seattle

Recently on a plane to Seattle, there was a girl sitting in my row with an empty seat between us. I thought, *I should pray for her. I should find out what's going on in her life.* I prayed, "God, give me an opportunity." But as we talked, it seemed that nothing was happening. There was only small talk, and, honestly, I chickened out.

So I arrived in Seattle to speak to a bunch of pastors about *courage*. That was the topic! I gave the message and got right back in the car, after only being there for a few hours, and went right back to the airport. I got on the plane and went to sit down in my seat—and guess who was sitting right next to me? The girl from earlier that day! We looked at each other and laughed. So I was able to tell her, "I don't think this is a coincidence. Let me tell you what the Lord put on my heart this morning but I was scared to do." God, by his grace, instead of having her sit one seat over, had her in the seat right next to me on the way home. Hopefully she was able to walk away that day seeing that it wasn't just about sitting next to some preacher but that God was pursuing her.

Answered Prayer in a Cab with a Muslim

I was in a cab with a Muslim one time, and I wanted to share Jesus with him. I asked him, "What do you believe? Help me understand because I've heard different things from different Muslims. I want to understand." And I asked, "Are you going to heaven? Are you sure? Tell me how you know this. Tell me how you know you're forgiven." He gave his spiel, and then I laid out what I believed. It went back and forth.

Then I started talking to him about knowing God. I told him, "When I pray, God answers me. It's the craziest thing. He actually listens and often answers!" I listed off several examples and told him the recent things God had been doing in my life.

"Does God do that for you?" I asked.

He answered, "Oh yeah."

As I was listening to him, I was thinking, *God, that's not supposed to happen!* I really was bothered by it, and we went on to another topic.

But a few minutes later he said, "Hey, you know earlier I said that God listens. I didn't mean that. Actually he doesn't." What a relief! It really was bothering me that he said God listened to him, and I was praying, "No, Lord, I am so confused here because I know I know you. I know you listen to me." It really confused me that a Muslim man would say that God answers his prayers too.

But then I love the fact that he was so honest and later came back and said, "Well, you know what? Actually he doesn't answer me like that." Christian, it is breathtaking that our God loves us, knows us, hears us, and answers our prayers.

Boasting in the Lord

Paul writes in 1 Corinthians 1:31, "Let the one who boasts, boast in the Lord." Do you know where he gets that? It's from Jeremiah 9:23–24: "Let not the wise man boast in his wisdom, let not the mighty man boast in his might, let not the rich man boast in his riches, but let him who boasts boast in this, that he understands and knows me.'"

You want to brag about something? Brag about the fact that you know God—and even better, that God knows you. Hopefully you're experiencing him in your everyday life, and you really believe these truths and these promises that we've been thinking about in Scripture to the point that when you pray, you don't doubt that God is listening to you. This may sound crazy, but he actually listens. He answers our prayers. The silly golf club. The girl on the airplane. The Muslim in the cab. This happens to me all the time. God knows me. He listens to me. Little, seemingly insignificant me—and you.

Don't boast about how much you know. Don't boast about your knowledge, your might, or anything else. Boast about being known by God. Right now, the God of the universe knows you. He loves you, and he calls you by name.

Does Your Life Look Like Jesus's?

To close this chapter, I was trying to think about the most loving thing I could say to you, based on 1 Corinthians 8:1–3, wanting to build you up and to think about you. I love you, and what knowledge I do have, and what giftedness I do have, I want to use it to build you up and give you a sense of encouragement. Christians are charged to encourage one another and stir one another up. So what can I say based on my love for you, and based on the knowledge that if you're in Christ, I'll see you one hundred years from now in heaven? Here's my closing thought.

Some of you have been studying Christ for years. You've been studying the life of Christ, the statements of Christ, and doctrines about Christ. You've been thinking hard about Christ and his work. You may have amassed great theological knowledge. But does your life look anything like his? Can you say, like Paul was able to say, "Be imitators of me, as I am of Christ" (1 Cor. 11:1)? Can you say, "Look at the way I'm living, and look at the way that I'm loving, and follow me"? Anyone can talk. A lot of people have knowledge—with the Internet it's easier than ever to load up on information. But what about your whole life? Hebrews 13:7 says, "Remember your leaders, those who spoke to you the word of God. Consider the outcome of *their way of life*, and imitate their faith." Look at *their lives*. Look at *how they lived*. Are you ready for others to do that to you? Do you look like Jesus? Do you act like Jesus? Do you love like Jesus?

Walking with Jesus

There was a missionary who spoke at our church years ago who had gone to Papua New Guinea and won a tribe to Jesus. It was a beautiful story. At the end, he mentioned the pivotal influence of his youth pastor, a man named Vaughn, who loved him and told him that his life was to be lived for the glory of God.

Then, the next week, we had another man come and talk about sponsoring kids, and when he was at the end of his presentation, he said, "Under God, I owe this all to the influence of my youth pastor Vaughn." So I asked and found out that these two guys had been in the same youth group.

The next week one of our church members who works with the Rescue Mission in inner-city Los Angeles spoke to us. No, he didn't mention Vaughn. But he had been in attendance the previous two weeks, and so I said to him after he was finished, "Wasn't it weird that those two guys the last two weeks both mentioned how much impact their youth pastor Vaughn had on them?"

He said, "Oh, I know Vaughn."

"Really? The same Vaughn?"

"Yeah." And he told me the story.

Vaughn is a pastor in San Diego and takes people into the dumps of Tijuana. "I spent a day with him," he said. "He ministers there in the dumps where kids are picking out of the garbage and are filthy dirty. As we walked the city, these kids came running up to him. And he would just love on them. He would hug them, and he had gifts for them. He'd have food for them. He'd figure out how to get them showers." He continued, "I just followed Vaughn around that whole day."

Then here's the amazing thing. He said, "Francis, it was eerie. The whole time I was walking with Vaughn I kept thinking, *If Jesus was on the earth, I think this is what it would feel like to walk with him.* Vaughn so loved everyone he ran into, and he told them about God and the gospel, and people were drawn to his love and his affection." Then he said, "The day I spent with Vaughn was the closest thing I've ever experienced to walking with Jesus."

What a compliment. *The day I spent with Vaughn was the closest I've ever experienced to walking with Jesus.* It made me think, *Would anyone in their right mind say that about me?*

Would anyone say that about you?

It made me realize that all this other stuff—like being smart or being a good speaker—is not the goal. Or if people say, "Wow, you know so much Bible," that's great, but at the end of the day, would they say, "Wow, it's weird hanging out with you. I mean, I read about Jesus and then I walk with you and it's, like, the same thing, the way you love so much till it hurts. You sacrifice and you give up. It's true humility. You're giving, giving, giving"?

Wasn't becoming more like Jesus supposed to be the goal of gaining all this knowledge about him in the first place? That's what I want. I don't want to be the best speaker in the world. Or the best writer. Or the most intelligent person on the planet. It simply doesn't matter. What do you want to be known for? I want to be known for being like Jesus.

A Closing Challenge to Thinkers

Thinkers, let's not fool ourselves: To "be conformed to the image of [Christ]" is what we were predestined for, right (Rom. 8:29)? We've been predestined to walk as Jesus walked. It's great if we have thought hard about Jesus and wrestled with doctrines such as predestination, but my prayer is that this information becomes true knowledge, and that we actually become like him, and that our knowledge doesn't make us arrogant so that we gloat about it and show off what we know. My prayer for me, and for you, is that everyone we come in contact with would feel our love for them and be built up. That they would see the fruit of our having said, "How can I lift them up with this knowledge that I have?"

Let's not fool ourselves and imagine that we know so much. Maybe we don't know anything at all. Maybe some of us have been using our knowledge to tear our brother down and hurt that brother for whom Christ died. Let's not be guilty of the Corinthian error.

So I'm asking God even right now as I write these final words that he would give me love for others. *Oh, God, let me believe what I'm saying.* And I hope that as you finish this chapter, you would think through your words and how you can build others up and think about others as brothers and sisters in Christ—so much so that when unbelievers see it, they will have a glimpse of God.

*   *   *

Father,
Help us to dwell on Christ. We want to become like him, Father. Give us love. I pray that my brothers and sisters reading this chapter have been built up and encouraged, believing they can do great things in Christ. I pray that they feel strengthened to love one another.

God, forgive us for the careless statements we make that may have destroyed or weakened our brothers and sisters and hurt them and not motivated them to greater ministry.

I thank you for the men and the women reading this chapter who have used their knowledge to build others up. Cause them to love you more and to become more like you.

God, we really want to become more like Jesus. More and more. Help us to see him not only as a great Savior but as a great role model of love. Make our lives really be conformed to his, and may people see Christ when they see our lives. May they see you when they see us love one another. Use our knowledge. May we think hard about your Word, and may we think hard about people. May we think hard about our brothers and sisters, and may we think hard about those who are lost and headed for an eternity apart from you.

In Jesus's name we pray.
Amen

Conclusion

Thinking for the Sake of Joy:
The Life of the Mind and the Love of God

JOHN PIPER

There are negative aims that we have for this book and positive ones—things we want to prevent and things we want to promote. The main positive aim is that you will embrace serious thinking as a way of loving God and people—that through the awakening and sharpening of your thinking, you will love God and love people more deeply and more fully and more unshakably. We will turn to that aim below. But let me mention first some of the negative aims of this book. These are things that we would like to prevent.

Eight Things We Hope This Book Will Help Prevent

1) *We hope that you will not be naïve about the depravity of the human mind—your mind.*

In 2 Corinthians 3:14, Paul says the mind is "hardened" (*epōrōthē*). In 1 Timothy 6:5, he calls the mind "depraved" (*diephtharmenōn*). In Ephesians 4:18, he says men are "darkened in their understanding, alienated from the life of God." In Romans 1:21, he says that thinking has become "futile" (*emaraiōthēsan*) and "foolish" (*asunetos*), because men "by their unrighteousness suppress the truth" (Rom. 1:18). He warns against being taken "captive by philosophy" (Col. 2:8). And he says in 1 Corinthians 1:21, "In the wisdom of God, the world did not know God through wisdom."

And so our first negative aim is that you would not be naïve about what we are up against. If there is a holy place for thinking in the Christian life, something dramatic has to happen to overcome these kinds of obstacles. We must be born again and continually renewed by the Holy Spirit.

2) *We hope that your mind will not be complicit in spiritual adultery.*

In Matthew 16:1–4, the Pharisees and Sadducees came to Jesus to test him and asked him to show them a sign from heaven. And in the way he answered them, he showed that their thinking was complicit in spiritual adultery. He said:

> When it is evening, you say, "It will be fair weather, for the sky is red." And in the morning, "It will be stormy today, for the sky is red and threatening." You know how to interpret the appearance of the sky, but you cannot interpret the signs of the times. An evil and adulterous generation seeks for a sign.

When it came to the weather, they were using their minds with Aristotelian precision:

> Premise one: Red skies at night mean fair weather tomorrow.
> Premise two: The sky is red tonight.
> Conclusion: Tomorrow it will be fair.

Exactly. Good thinking. Good use of the mind. "You know how to interpret the appearance of the sky."

But then Jesus says, "But you cannot interpret the signs of the times." You cannot see me for who I am. You cannot see that these are the last days. The Messiah is here. The kingdom of God is breaking in. And your minds are incapable of grasping this. You "cannot interpret the signs." Good mind for the weather. Blind mind for the Bridegroom.

God is the husband of Israel. He has come to her in Jesus. Surely she knows her husband! Surely her mental faculties will work as well to know her beloved as to know the weather? Surely she will not stand before her husband and say: "Prove it. Give me a sign that you are my beloved." Surely her weather-knowing mind will know her husband.

No. And why not? Jesus gives the answer in verse 4: "An evil and *adulterous* generation seeks for a sign." Adulterous? What does that mean? It means their Messiah, their husband, was not what they wanted. Their hearts preferred other lovers (see Luke 16:14; 18:9; Matt. 6:5). They were spiritual adulterers.

And what was the effect on their minds? Blindness. So beware of letting your heart become so enamored by other lovers that your mind cannot know your king when he comes. Beware of making your minds complicit in spiritual adultery.

3) *We hope that you will not be cagy or slippery with your mind.*

Jesus will not tolerate caginess in any relationship with himself. He will not deal with people who use their minds to be shifty with the truth (Matt. 21:23–27). The chief priests ask him, "By what authority are you doing these things?" He could see their devious hearts. So he said, "I also will ask you one question, and if you tell me the answer, then I also will tell you by what authority I do these things. The baptism of John, from where did it come? From heaven or from man?"

Instead of being forthright and clear and upfront, they become cagy. They used their minds to become slippery. They say, "If we say, 'From heaven,' he will say to us, 'Why then did you not believe him?' But if we say, 'From man,' we are afraid of the crowd, for they all hold that John was a prophet." So they answered Jesus, "We do not know."

Jesus will not talk to people like that. He said to them, "Neither will I tell you by what authority I do these things." We hope that you will not be cagy or slippery with your mind, but that you will be like Paul when he said, "We refuse to practice cunning or to tamper with God's word, but by the open statement of the truth we would commend ourselves to everyone's conscience in the sight of God" (2 Cor. 4:2).

4) *We hope that you will not be romantic about the benefits of ignorance.*

There is an odd notion that, if we use our minds to grow in our knowledge of God, mystery will diminish and with it a sense of wonder and reverence. I call this notion odd for two reasons. One is that no matter how many millions of ages I use my mind to know more and more of God's majesty, his glories will never be in danger of being exhausted. What is not yet known of God by finite creatures will always be limitless. You honor this truth more by shameless growth in the knowledge of God.

And the second reason I find the notion odd that thinking about God and knowing more and more of God jeopardize our worship of God, is that without knowing him we can't worship in a way that honors him. God is not honored when people get excited about how little they know of him.

Ignorance of God has never been the ground of true worship. While we don't know all, and never will know all, we know something, because God has chosen to reveal himself. And he is honored when our worship is based on what he has revealed, not on what he hasn't.

So don't be romantic about the benefits of ignorance. Be more enthralled by the God you know than by the God you don't know.

FACINATE

5) *We hope that you will not be children in your thinking, but mature.*

Paul said, "Brothers, do not be children in your thinking. Be infants in evil, but in your thinking be mature" (1 Cor. 14:20). There is a kind of thinking that Paul calls "mature" and a kind that children do. He wants us to grow up in our thinking, which is what I hope this book leads to. I mention this goal mainly to make the next one stand out.

6) *We hope that you will be children in your thinking.*

I know this is not a negative goal, but it puts the previous one in such stark relief that it belongs here. And in a sense, it is a negative goal because it's the flipside of saying: *We hope you will not be "wise and understanding."* Jesus said in Luke 10:21, "I thank you, Father, Lord of heaven and earth, that you have hidden these things from the *wise and understanding* and revealed them to little *children*; yes, Father, for such was your gracious will." So we don't want you to be "wise and understanding" but "children."

The wise and understanding are proud and self-sufficient in their knowledge. They use their minds not to know God and submit to God and love God but to exalt themselves and seek the praise of men and escape God. But the "children" are those with a childlike mind, a humble mind, a trusting, God-dependent mind. They look to God with humble expectancy, and he reveals himself to them.

So we hope you will not be children in your thinking, and that you will be children in your thinking. And I say it like that because it is precisely by seeing such things in the Bible that it is made clear that God wants us to think! He wants us to ask: In what sense is it good to be like children, and in what sense is it not? And then to use our minds to pursue the biblical answer.

CONCLUSIVE-

7) *We do not want you to view thinking as unnecessary in knowing God or as decisive in knowing God.*

It is necessary, but it is not decisive. God's sovereign illumination is decisive. The key text behind the entire conference, as I first conceived it, that led to this book, is 2 Timothy 2:7. Paul says to Timothy, "*Think* over what I say, for the Lord will *give* you understanding in everything." Think! It's a command. Why think? "Because [key word 'for'!] the Lord will give you understanding." The ground of our thinking is God's giving understanding. This has been one of the most influential texts in my thinking biblically about thinking.

We don't want you to undervalue biblically the necessity of thinking. At least ten times in the book of Acts, Luke says that Paul's strategy was to "reason" with people in his effort to convert them to Jesus and build them up (Acts 17:2, 4, 17; 18:4, 19; 19:8, 9; 20:7, 9; 24:25). The role of the mind in thinking seriously about God's revelation was simply huge for Paul.

But it was not decisive in coming to faith or in knowing God. Necessary, but not decisive. "*Think* over what I say, for *the Lord will give you understanding* in everything." So many people swerve off the road to one side of this verse or the other. Some stress, "Think over what I say." They emphasize the indispensable role of reason and thinking. And they often minimize the decisive supernatural role of God in making the mind able to see and embrace the truth. Others stress the second half of the verse: "for the Lord will give you understanding in everything." They emphasize the futility of reason without God's illumining work.

But Paul will not be divided that way. And this book is a plea to you that you not force that division either. We hope you will embrace both human thinking and divine illumination. For Paul, it was not *either-or* but *both-and*. "*Think* over what I say, for *the Lord will give you understanding* in everything."

And notice the little word "for." This means that the promise of God to give us understanding is the *ground* of our thinking, not the substitute for it. Paul does not say, "God gives you understanding, so don't waste your time thinking over what I say." Nor does he say, "Think hard over what I say because it all depends on you, and God does not illumine the mind."

No. He emphatically makes God's gift of illumination the ground of our effort to understand. There is no reason to believe that a person who *thinks* without prayerful trust in God's gift of understanding will get it. And there is no reason to believe that a person who waits for God's gift of understanding without thinking about his Word will get it either. *Both-and*. Not *either-or*.

8) *The last negative goal for this book that I will mention is that yours will not be a proud, loveless mind.*

Here I underscore Francis Chan's embodied exposition of 1 Corinthians 8:1–3 in the previous chapter. Paul says, "Now concerning food offered to idols: we know that 'all of us possess knowledge.' This 'knowledge' puffs up, but love builds up. If anyone imagines that he knows something, he does not yet know as he ought to know. But if anyone loves God, he is known by God."

One thing is clear: knowledge that is loveless is not true knowledge. It's imaginary knowledge, no matter how factual it is: "If anyone imagines that he knows something, he does not yet know as he ought to know. But if anyone loves God, he is known by God." Knowing as we ought to know is a knowing for the sake of loving. Loving God and loving people.

So our main aim negatively is that you not finish this book with a proud and loveless mind. Which leads me now to the main positive aim of the book, that you embrace serious thinking as a means of loving God and people.

What We Hope This Book Will Awaken and Increase:
Thinking for the Sake of Loving

The main focus here is the Great Commandment. What did Jesus mean when he said, "You shall love the Lord your God with all your mind"? You recall the story. A Pharisee asked Jesus, "Teacher, which is the great commandment in the Law?" He answered, "You shall love the Lord your God with all your heart and with all your soul and with all your mind. This is the great and first commandment. And a second is like it: You shall love your neighbor as yourself" (Matt. 22:36–39).

So the greatest commandment in the Bible is to love God. And Jesus says to do this with our mind. What does it mean to love God "with all your mind"? I'll give you my answer and then try to show you from the context where I got this.

When Jesus says, "Love God will all your mind," I take him to mean that *our thinking should be wholly engaged to do all it can to awaken and express the heartfelt fullness of treasuring God above all things.*

Not a Mere Decision

Notice two things about this understanding. One is that I am taking "loving God" to mean mainly *treasuring* God. The other is that thinking (the mind) is a means to that end. In other words, it's an experience of cherishing, delighting, admiring, and valuing. It's not a thought about God or a work for God. It's the sort of thing Paul meant when he said, "I count everything as loss because of the surpassing worth of knowing Christ Jesus my Lord" (Phil. 3:8). It's about treasuring worth. Love for God is an affair of the affections. Ideas and thoughts and thinking are crucial (as we will see), but they are not what love *is*. Thinking is for the sake of loving. It's a means to loving. It's not what love *is*. That's my interpretation.

It's not a mere decision any more than your treasuring the beauty of a sunset is a mere decision. You don't decide to find beauty compelling. It happens to you. Loving God means that God is our supreme treasure and pleasure. We prefer above all else to know him and see him and be with him and be like him.

Loving God as Treasuring Him

Now let me try to unpack it and defend it. Why do I define loving God mainly as treasuring God? Why do I believe that love for God is most essentially an experience of the affections, not mere thought or mere behavior?

When Jesus said, "If you love me, you will keep my commandments" (John 14:15), he emphatically did not say that keeping his commandments is what love *is*. He distinguished the two and made commandment keeping the evidence of loving him, not the definition of loving him.

And when Jesus says the second commandment (keeping God's commandment to love our neighbor as ourselves), he emphatically did not say that the second commandment was interchangeable with the first one. It is like it. It is not it. Loving God is not defined by loving neighbor. It is demonstrated by loving neighbor. "He who does not love his brother whom he has seen cannot love God whom he has not seen" (1 John 4:20). But they are not identical.

Actions Are Not the Essence of Worship

Or consider the way Jesus talks about the heart worshiping him. "This people honors me with their lips, but their heart is far from me; in vain do they worship me" (Mark 7:6–7). In other words, external actions—even religious ones directed toward God—are *not* the essence of worship. They are not the essence of love. What happens in the heart is essential. The external behaviors will be pleasing to God when they flow from a heart that freely treasures God above all things.

Or consider what Jesus says about loving and hating God in Matthew 6:24. "No one can serve two masters, for either he will hate the one and love the other, or he will be devoted to the one and despise the other. You cannot serve God and money." The opposite of loving God is "hating" and "despising." These are strong emotional words. They imply that the positive counterpart is also a strong emotion. So loving God is a strong inward emotion, not a mere outward action.

Loving Is Treasuring

So I take loving God in the Great Commandment to mean most essentially *treasuring* God—valuing him, cherishing him, admiring him, desiring him. Therefore, loving him with all our mind means that *our mind—our thinking—is not what does the loving but what fuels the loving. Loving God with the mind means our mind does all it can to awaken and express our treasuring God above all things.*

If we equate loving God with thinking rightly about God, we jeopardize the very reality of love. If you say that fire and fuel are the same, you may not order the wood. Then the fire goes out. The fire is not the wood. But for the sake of the fire, you exert yourself to provide the wood. And for the sake of love, you exert your mind and provide knowledge.

We cannot love God without knowing God; and the way we know God is by the Spirit-enabled use of our minds. So to "love God with all your mind" means engaging all your powers of thought to know God as fully as possible in order to treasure him for all he is worth.

Where Should We Focus?

And where should our mind focus in order to know God most fully and deeply? We could focus on nature because the heavens are telling the glory of God (Ps. 19:1). We could focus on the human soul for we are made in the image of God. We could focus on the history of Israel because God calls Israel "my glory" (Isa. 46:13). We could focus on the life of Christ because he is "the radiance of the glory of God and the exact imprint of his nature" (Heb. 1:3). Or we could come to the event where more of God is revealed than any other event in history, the death of his Son. All the other revelations of God in Christ are like rays of sun breaking through the clouds. But the death of Christ for sinners was like a bolt of lightning.

If we want to spend our minds to the fullest in knowing God to the fullest so that we can love him to the fullest, this is where we will focus. And when our thinking begins to focus on this event, something strange happens. The light of God's glory that we meet at the cross is so strong and so bright as to make all self-exalting thinking look foolish.

Thinking about the Cross

"God [has] made foolish the wisdom of the world," Paul says, "For . . . in the wisdom of God, the world did not know God through wisdom" (1 Cor. 1:20–21). The human wisdom that cannot know God—the human thinking that cannot fathom the cross—is self-exalting wisdom, man-centered wisdom, sin-denying wisdom. Of this wisdom Paul says:

- "God [has] made foolish the wisdom of the world" (1 Cor. 1:20).
- God "will destroy the wisdom of the wise" (1 Cor. 1:19).
- "The foolishness of God is wiser than men" (1 Cor. 1:25).
- "The word of the cross is folly to those who are perishing" (1 Cor. 1:18).

But none of that means we shouldn't use our minds to think about the cross. There is a right thinking about the cross. There is a true wisdom in the cross. Paul said, "Among the mature we do impart wisdom" (1 Cor. 2:6). The difference between the wisdom that the cross destroys and the wisdom that the cross awakens is the difference between self-exalting wisdom and Christ-exalting wisdom. True wisdom sees the glory of God in the cross. False wisdom sees the cross as foolishness because it threatens our pride.

There is no other object of knowledge in the universe that exposes proud, man-exalting thinking like the cross does. Only humble, Christ-exalting thinking can survive in the presence of the cross. The effect of the cross on our thinking is not to cut off thinking about God but to confound boasting in the presence of God. The cross does not nullify thinking; it purifies thinking.

Our Prayer

So as you come to the end of this book, our prayer is:

1) that you will not be naïve about the depravity of your mind;
2) that you will not be mentally complicit in spiritual adultery;
3) that you will not be cagy or slippery with your mind;
4) that you will not have romantic notions about the benefits of an ignorant mind;
5) that you will not be children in your thinking in the wrong way;
6) but that you will be children in your thinking in the good way;

7) that you will not view thinking as unnecessary in knowing God or as decisive in knowing God, but as necessary and not decisive;

8) and that yours will not be a proud, loveless mind in relation to other people.

But I pray that you will love God with all your mind—that you will engage your thinking as fully as possible for the sake of knowing God as fully as possible, for the sake of treasuring God as fully as possible. That you will employ your mind to provide your heart with as much fuel for the fires of love as it can possibly deliver.

To that end may the cross of Christ, the deepest, highest, clearest revelation of God in history, be the focus of your thinking. There is no other place where you can see him more clearly or love him more dearly. Here is the place where your thinking will be most deeply purified, and the worth of God will be most fully magnified. Amen.

*   *   *

A Prayer for Love through Thinking

Father,

You have made it plain in your word that the greatest commandment is to love—to love you above all and to love our neighbor as ourselves. My prayer is that everything in this book will serve that end. Would you grant that everyone who reads would think more clearly, more humbly, more biblically, more coherently, more maturely, and more deeply, to the end that you might be known more truly and loved more ardently? And grant that our love for you—our worshipful joy in your wonders and your ways—would expand daily into the lives of those who suffer God-less emptiness, whether rich or poor. And may your name be magnified as supremely valuable by the truth in our minds, the affections of our hearts, the words of our lips, and the sacrifices of our hands.

In Jesus's name.
Amen

A Conversation with the Contributors

THABITI ANYABWILE, AL MOHLER, FRANCIS CHAN, AND JOHN PIPER, WITH DAVID MATHIS

The following is a lightly edited transcription of a panel discussion held on October 2, 2010, at the Desiring God National Conference, where the chapters of this book were originally delivered. David Mathis's questions are in bold.

The greatest object to which we can turn our thinking is the fullest, richest, deepest revelation of God in the person and work of his Son Jesus. Thabiti, we thought it might be fitting to turn our minds there at the outset of this panel. Would you lead us in rehearsing the great message of the gospel?

THABITI ANYABWILE: The gospel is literally "good news." It's an announcement—a joyful, happy message sent from the courts of heaven to us subjects below. One way of summarizing it is in these four categories: God, sin, Jesus, faith. The gospel is news that demands a response, unlike evening news on television. What's announced to us in the gospel is that:

- There is a God. He's the only God. There is none like him. He is holy and righteous, infinite, all-powerful, all-wise. He is the creator of everything. We are created; therefore, we are owned. As creatures, we owe this creator worship and love and adoration and honor and praise. And this holy God, who has made us in his image for fellowship with him, is actually angry with us in his righteousness and holiness because . . .

- We all are sinners. We all have disobeyed God. We all have dishonored God. We all have turned away from God. Al Mohler writes so helpfully in his chapter about Romans 1 that we all have been darkened in our own minds, and we are hostile toward God as sinners. But God is not only holy and righteous, and justly wrathful toward sinners, but he also is a God of love.

- So God sent his Son, Jesus, who took on our flesh, our likeness, and lived a fully human and perfectly righteous life before God to satisfy the holy requirements of God and died an agonizing death, suffering the wrath of God to pay the penalty for our sins on Calvary's cross, so that the wrath of God would be satisfied in him and turned away from us. Jesus was buried and three days later resurrected. He ascended into heaven, sits now at the Father's right hand, and is coming again. Jesus in his perfect righteousness supplies all the righteousness that sinners will ever need, and his death satisfies the demands of God against sinners for their rebellion against him.

- Lastly, this message demands a response: all who *repent of their sin* and *trust by faith in Jesus* have his righteousness counted to them in him and have their sin nailed to the cross with him so that they bear it no more. They are eternally forgiven. They are eternally cleansed. A miracle happens: they are made new creatures in Jesus, and in him through faith connected to all of the benefits of Christ, including the promises of everlasting life and everlasting fellowship with God and the joy of basking in his love and in his glory for all eternity.

That's the happy news. The good news—the gospel.

And so the appeal I make to you, the appeal that God is making through me to you, is that, having heard this message, you would put your faith in Jesus and trust yourself fully to him, call upon his name—everyone who calls on his name will be saved. That's my hope for you. And I pray that you would not let this day pass without discovering more of what it means to trust in Jesus, to repent of your sins, and to follow him in the obedience of faith, and so be saved.

Francis, how has God been working on you through the messages that we've heard from Rick Warren, R. C. Sproul, Al Mohler, and Thabiti Anyabwile?

FRANCIS CHAN: I am almost sick to my stomach after Al's message. A lot of it is my own sin. After hearing Al speak, I was hoping to find someone else here on my level. I thank God for what Al explained and all the research he has done. On the one hand, I feel more courageous than ever, because I have my brothers here striving side by side with me for the sake of the gospel. On the other hand, I have been sitting here praying, *God, what else is there to say? They've said everything! They've said things I didn't know, that I would never know to say. I could never do that. I could never do that.* John Piper said it so well after Rick Warren's message: "Wow, I couldn't do that." With each speaker we get to see how God uniquely created him. I am very encouraged and am so thrilled that I am on a team with these guys, because it makes me feel stronger. Isn't it the same for you? I am so glad that they can think at that level. I'm so glad that they can help us defend the gospel. It is a comfort that guys like this are on our side.

So there is that encouragement there, but there is this other side where I'm sure some others are struggling. I say, *Lord, what do I have to offer? And yet I trust your Word. I know your Word tells me that you created me. So I'm not a screw-up.* It's like Moses when he says, "Oh, I don't speak good." And God says, "Wait now. Who made your mouth?" And so humility is not saying, "Oh, I can't offer anything to these contributors." Humility is saying, "No, God, you've gifted me and filled me with your Spirit. So there's something I have to offer." And that has me wrestling, and it's a fight to believe the truth of God's Word when you are battling your own flesh or your own insecurities.

There was a period in my life when I was almost anti-scholarship, because after seminary and after studying for years (and being around a lot of brilliant people), I was almost made to feel worthless, like I had nothing to offer. And there have been times I have even thought about quitting ministry and going back to school to study some more, because I'm not at that level. And what I have loved is the gracious way that these other contributors have helped the rest of us who don't think as well or haven't thought as deeply in that area. We all have a part in the body of Christ, and we all need each other, and we shouldn't try to be each other but be who God has made us. I haven't always gotten that from people who are more intelligent than

I. And a lot of the writings of these other contributors in the last few years have really renewed my attitude toward scholarship, because I have been able to see that there is a way to study that can help other people and build them up and lift them up. There is a way to think that will actually make you more passionate about Jesus rather than just cold and arrogant. To make you have affections for him, for people, and for the body of Christ.

Thabiti, you are a formidable thinker and local church pastor, and it's a fairly recent pastorate. How would you counsel a congregant who feels too intellectually stretched by your sermons to stay with you and grow in the life of the mind?

THABITI ANYABWILE: That's a good question. Answering it might get me in trouble back home. At the end of the day, I don't know how to do anything but be me. And as a preacher, I'm mainly trying to remember to preach for an audience of one—to glorify Jesus—but I'm also trying to serve his people. So one of the things I pray for in my own preaching is clarity. I don't feel like I am a particularly good illustrator, for example, which can help clarity, if done appropriately. There is power in clarity and simplicity and forceful thought.

So I invite my people to give me feedback as to that. When I hear such a complaint from one of my hearers, I ask whether I'm really hearing *"You weren't clear,"* or if I am hearing, *"Bring that particular idea, that doctrinal point, home in terms of application,"* or if I am hearing, *"Yeah, actually you're stretching me right now."* I encourage folks that it is good to be stretched. Sometimes I think we are quite complacent in our thinking. We have a proxy for what it means to be mature spiritually, which I think is a bad proxy. Many Christians think if they've been in the church a long time and they haven't heard something before, then the new thing that they're hearing is a novelty and maybe needs to be discarded, because, after all, they've been in church a long time and have certain habits down, and so therefore are mature in their thinking as a Christian or living as a Christian. I want to push back against that. Yes, I want to be gracious and loving, but I don't want my people to settle. I want them to love the Lord their God with all their mind, heart, and strength. So I want to be approachable and receive feedback and critique that helps the preaching. I want to make sure that my preaching isn't about being seen to be clever but is being helpful and useful in the right ways as I expound the Scripture.

Al, in your message you talked about the shifting ways of thinking from the pre-modern era, to the modern, and now to the postmodern, and you mentioned the honest confession of intellectual prejudice as one of the goods that comes with postmodern thinking. You also highlighted for us many of the dangers in postmodern thinking. Would there be other goods in postmodern thinking that you would point to that are of use for gospel advance?

AL MOHLER: Indeed. And as a matter of fact, a lot of what we think about in terms of cross-cultural conversation and communication is very indebted to postmodern insights about the social location of meaning. The fact is that meaning is culturally situated. It's very linguistic. That's why translating language to language is never a one-to-one thing, and it's a whole conceptual world endeavor.

There's another one, quite frankly, that's a key insight. The hard antirealist, postmodernist guys that are supposed to have their profiles in the evangelical post office—those were the ones who said all truth is socially constructed in order to serve the interests of people in power. We know that's not true. We also know it's largely true. Which is to say we understand that, in a sinful world, we actually have a theological reason for understanding why that happens. We don't just look at it and say, "Oh, isn't it awful that that's the way it happens, and let's deconstruct it." We look at it and say, "No, that's true." What the apostle Paul does is deconstruct alternative worldviews. And that's exactly what Israel is called to do in the Old Testament. We can't accept the antirealism. We can't accept the hostility to truth. But we can say to someone, "If you've been burned by all of the false claims to truth and all of the racism and ethnocentrism and all the rest that's been a part of Western civilization or some other, then it's going to come very, very naturally to you to believe that all truth emerges from that same kind of sinful claim; all truth claims emerge from that same kind of power grab." And this is where we come back and say that the gospel is the great truth, the infinitely true truth claim that is God's message of grace.

The unregenerate mind, as the Reformers said, can know many things accurately, and where it gets it right, we need to recognize that's judgment if we've been thinking wrongly in order that we can get to the truth of the gospel and actually be truer truth tellers, more accurate truth tellers. One of the great challenges for evangelicals, and I mean true evangelicals—those who love the gospel—is going to be how to understand the cross-cultural communication challenges that we're going to live with till Jesus comes and how to be faithful in the midst of that. It's going to take a lot of us thinking, all of us thinking, as faithfully as the Lord would lead us to think together.

John, as we've seen, there is a relationship between thinking, feeling, and doing. You were significantly honored here today. [John was presented with a book titled *For the Fame of God's Name: Essays in Honor of John Piper*, edited by Sam Storms and Justin Taylor, with chapters written by twenty-seven of his ministry friends.] Walk us through, if you would, how we should think through being honored. There appear to be dangers on either side. How have you learned over the years to walk through such moments of honor?

JOHN PIPER: Oh, my. Probably the first thing to say is that God is in charge of keeping his people humble, not us. The Bible does say that we should humble ourselves under the mighty hand of God, but as in almost all other things, "command what you will and give what you command." So, we can expect that God will deal roughly with us, if he has to, in order to remind us that we are not God and that we are desperately in need of him.

Perhaps it is no accident that I received this book of essays in the middle of a leave of absence taken because of pain. Is that an accident that it worked out that way? The editors and contributors have been working on the book for three years, they said. There are issues in my family and my wider family and my soul that are such that I asked for this leave so I could step back and look at all of them and work on all of them. I felt, as I sat there watching the surprise presentation of the book, that these folks don't know me well enough. They don't know what goes on in our living room and bedroom and kitchen. I know. My wife knows and my children know. And so I feel the sense of disjunction between public praise and private imperfections. And this seems to be God's doing. He forms that.

Then there are these natural limitations that the people closest around me know that I have. And I don't know why God has been pleased to release influence through me the way that he has when I look at the limitations. I can't read faster than I can talk. Everybody thinks I'm a scholar—I'm not a scholar! The contributors are going to wake up and think, *What did we just do?* I have learned to navigate my limitations and just do the few things I can do as well as I can. And I'm always thinking about what I can't do. I wake up in the morning and think of what I can't do.

So God fits us with weaknesses. He leads us through the valley of the shadow of death. He leads us in his providence, yes, even in and out of sin, and does what he has to do to break us. So that's the first principle. God is in charge of keeping us humble, and he loves us so much, as Hebrews 12 says, that if we think we are his child but we have not yet been disciplined, we may be bastards. Those are strong words in Hebrews 12. If you haven't been spanked hard enough to come to blood, then maybe you're not even a child. That's the way he works.

The second thing I would say—I'll say it first from a wider angle and then from a more focused angle—is that we leaders here believe in a certain vision of God's sovereign grace. There is not a thing in you or me that inclined God to choose us for himself. Nothing. There is not a thing in you or me that inclined God to cause us to be born again. Nothing. There is not a thing in you or me that secures our eternal destiny. Nothing. It is totally free. This is our theology—unconditional election, unconditional regeneration, unconditional propitiation, conditional justification, by faith alone—and that faith is a gift. Our theology is meant to flatten us. First Corinthians 1:27–31 says:

> God chose what is foolish in the world to shame the wise; God chose what is weak in the world to shame the strong; God chose what is

low and despised in the world, even things that are not, to bring to nothing things that are, so that no human being might boast in the presence of God. And because of him you are in Christ Jesus, who became to us wisdom from God, righteousness and sanctification and redemption, so that, as it is written, "Let the one who boasts, boast in the Lord."

Salvation is designed in a way as to cut the legs out from under all human boasting. It's about smashing human pride and getting glory for God. That's the big picture, the wider angle.

The more focused angle is Christ crucified. The most important event in human history is the death of the Son of God. What's the meaning of the death of the Son of God? It means I am unspeakably lost. It took that much—the death of God's own Son!—to save me. Anybody that lives near the cross isn't going to put his thumbs in his armpits, swing his elbows, and strut. Such a person is not going to brag about his stuff. He is not going to talk a lot about his achievements. He looks at that incredible horror—the Son of God on the cross—and sees it as a picture of how corrupt we are.

And the cross has another message—and it's good news. That's how much I'm loved. And it's free. *The* biggest challenge theologically and experientially for us is to feel loved unworthily, to get up in the morning and be thrilled to be alive and to be thrilled to know God totally undeservingly. That's the challenge, because we're wired to want to feel thrilled because we got a book or had a conference or gave a message. There is the constant clawing at my ego to find my meaning and my significance in other people's reckoning of what I've done.

So these contributors to this book in my honor are setting me up terribly. Right? But, like David said, we have to learn to deal with it. So you're watching me process this thing.

In sum, here are the three things. God is going to humble you whether you want him to or not. He's lovingly going to flatten you. Your marriage may go into pieces. Or your kids might go whacko on you. Or you may get cancer, or lose your job—God will do whatever he has to do, even flatten you, so that you are desperate before him. And then, secondly, he works through books like this and movements and other people to get us a theology with him so massively at the center that it no longer occurs to us to put ourselves there. And then, third, God takes us to the cross over and over and over again to remind us how un-save-able we are apart from that horrific crucifixion and how much we are amazingly loved.

There is just no escape from this battle, and so we must press on and pray hard for each other.

THABITI ANYABWILE: John, it is so freeing to hear you talk about being *unworthy and loved*, because when there is a sense of love attached to our worthiness, that is slavery—because then we find ourselves on this treadmill of trying to keep our worthiness up and at a level where we can fabricate the feeling of love. But to maintain that sense of being *unworthy and loved*, to be rightly abased, to have the idol of self smashed, that frees us to rejoice in our unworthiness, knowing that God loves us. That is so liberating. That is so wonderful.

At this conference, there has been a lot of talk, and rightfully so, about the life of the mind as it relates to the written Word of God—*and* at this conference we have seen several short video clips. How would you describe the role of audio and video, perhaps especially over the last ten-plus years, as it relates to the life of the mind and the development and sharpening of our minds?

AL MOHLER: I'm thankful for it. I think there are many things that can be extremely well (even beautifully) communicated by means of video—and audio with the video—but there is a certain power to the image, and that is biblically understood—and it can be a dangerous power. There is a recent book entitled *The Rise of the Image and the Fall of the Word*. That is devastating. "The fall of the word" is not what we Christians are about. This is partly because the image is far more susceptible to manipulation and to lying than the word, actually, because the image can be so easily attached to the emotions in ways that make it invisible to us. We are moved visually by things we don't want to be moved by, and we detect it in ourselves. We see something on television or especially a Hollywood movie that moves us, and we feel our emotions being pulled away from the truth. And that is a big danger.

But this is a visual age, and it seems we are actually kind of reverting to a pre-verbal, pre-linguistic age in many parts of the society. If you want to reach an awful lot of the people whom we know and love, then video is a powerful way to do it. But for Christians, let me make this plea: the image cannot replace the printed word, because the discipline of the printed word is a discipline of reading that requires a certain concentration, certain habits of the mind and habits of the heart that are not required by video.

Just last week I had to take two days away. Those days are very rare and precious. I had some writing that had to be done, and I had an opportunity between two trips to take two days just to write. I took a complete digital vacation, and I want to say to you, the digital natives, we need to wean ourselves at times off of video and audio and act like we are in a monastic cell, cut off from all culture and meaning, according to our peers, living as if we are our own parent and have grounded ourselves, because it is going to take that kind of discipline to be able to read certain things, much less to write certain things. And our souls need it. The apostle Paul told Timothy to bring the books and the parchments. I know, I know—he might say DVDs and iPod in some modern translations, but it is not the same thing.

I think we are living in a time in which it is very safe and important for us in the stewardship of media and communication opportunities to say we need to be good at media. The stuff that is produced for video, even for advertising new books, can be outstanding. I saw the video advertisement Desiring God did for John's book *Think* and thought, *People need to see that, because there are people who are going to see the video and be drawn into the book.* That's what I want. I want to see video draw people into deeper engagement with the written word.

JOHN PIPER: The main reason why we must always be a people devoting thought to the written word is that the Bible exists. Just let it sink in on you that the Bible exists. God did not do it any other way, and we are "stuck" with it till he comes back. That's the way it is. It's not a choice. Christians don't have a choice. God inspired the Bible. The Bible is in Greek and Hebrew, translated into other languages. Reading is an act of thinking. I have a whole chapter in the *Think* book just to show what I mean by thinking—and what I mean is *reading*. Reading happens either poorly or well, and when you read well, you are thinking. So the Bible mandates a focus on the written word, and it mandates thinking.

Here's the catch: the Bible commands preaching, which isn't written. It's seen and heard. Why? Why does it say in 2 Timothy 4:2, "Preach the word"? Because there is something more, something more in the Bible that people need. God has wired sheep to be fed not only by the distribution of books. Sheep are to be fed by shepherds who talk to them, because shepherds are alive, have wives and children and pain, feelings and passions and sorrows. And the people live there, and they need to see truth coming through that everyday life. That's why [we are to engage in] both the written word and the seen-and-heard preaching.

So we have the Bible that will never go away, this side of heaven. That was God's choice, and I think he didn't choose it because they didn't have videos back then, but he chose it because he created our minds, which learn how to do what they are supposed to do not mainly by listening but mainly by reading.

Now that has huge implications for pre-literate cultures. I would love to really go into this, because I have talked to Ajith Fernando, for example, about how he does expository preaching among pre-literate, nonreading peoples. And he says the Bible is crucial in doing it there. But enough. The Bible is a book. The book must be read either by the teachers or the students, and to be read, it must be thought about. And the Bible commands more than reading. It commands speaking.

AL MOHLER: Can I just add a word to that? The Scripture principle is so central to us. God gave us a word, first of all, the incarnate Word—we would say supremely an incarnate Word and then the written Word. And our dependence on the written Word just as John said, will not pass away in this life. Now, there are some interesting studies that have been done lately about multiplicities of meaning. It is hard enough to nail meaning down. Let's admit that. But if you compare what it means to try to get people to agree on what a text means and agreeing on what, say, a movie means, there is tremendous documentation that we are not talking about a slight difference. Just think of you and four or five friends going to see a movie and trying to agree what it was about, as if your life depended on it, versus a text. In our fallen state, the text is hard enough; the video is impossible. And it is important for us to understand that, in a fallen world, images have tremendous potential, but the potential might be more to make things interesting than to make things clear, and that is where we Christians want to be really careful.

Thabiti, I sensed a point of tension in your message, and perhaps you recognize this, between Islam not being able to be established in this country and yet there being "freedom of religion" in this country. So you encouraged us to fight for that freedom of religion, and advocate for the freedom of religion, yet also to advocate for "nonestablishment." However, Islam is not a religion that will take the freedom of religion without the establishment. Is there more that can be said there? Is Islam in this country "stuck"?

THABITI ANYABWILE: That's a great question. Thank you. Well, I do think there is a certain sense in which, yes, Islam is "stuck," but it is not a sense in which that stuck-ness is different from the Christian who is stuck, or the Jew who is stuck. We don't live in a theocracy, and I think the experiment historically of the wedding of church and state, or religion and state, has been disastrous for the state and the church. I think any reading of history teaches us that. And so what I am led to believe is actually, again, that there was a kindness of the Lord in the framing of our own sort of legal framework that prohibits, on the one hand, the establishment of religion and guarantees, on the other hand, the free exercise.

So what does that mean? I think it sets a context where we have to work it out, and I think it sets a context where we have to be intelligent about not advantaging or privileging particular perspectives (and I am speaking here primarily in religious terms), while at the same time not hindering or squashing others insofar as we protect basic liberties that are also spoken of in that document.

So, yes, we would be saying to Islam, and to Christianity, and to Hinduism, and Buddhism, and Judaism, and every other religious system, that we will not enshrine their point of view, religious practices, and religious precepts as the law of the land, which would violate what I think is one of the most basic human liberties, which is, again, the freedom of religion to worship God according to conscience. But at the same time, we will work to protect that liberty, that freedom, that ability to worship God according to the dictates of conscience.

So there is a dance there, and I think it is a good dance. I think it is the right dance, and I think we say to our Muslim neighbors and friends, "Welcome to the country, enjoy the freedoms here, let us love you as neighbors, let us show you hospitality. We would love to learn more and to engage and to talk more. We would not support the country becoming something other than what it is framed to be." And I think it is incumbent upon us perhaps, and certainly me, to be a better student of the Constitution, history, and law that we might be better stewards of that tension, of that balance, which I think is at this point, at least, a good and right tension.

Francis, you referenced earlier a previous anti-intellectual or anti-scholarship strain in your past, and yet at your previous church, Cornerstone, you founded a Bible College. Can you tell us how you went from some anti-scholarship sentiments to the founding of an institution for scholarship at the church?

FRANCIS CHAN: Yes. It happened when I began to encounter men who loved the Word of God—and it's still bothering me that John said he's not a scholar. Does that drive anyone else here crazy? Because, John, if you are not a scholar, then what in the world am I? John, I don't know if you remember when I first met you. You were speaking at Azusa Pacific University. I had spoken the day before and asked the faculty, "Can I drive him to the airport?" I just wanted to spend time with you.

And I remember in the car almost apologizing for not being a writer. I had tried to write at that time, and I just could not write. And I felt that anyone who knew as much about the Scriptures as he would want me to know just as much, or I was failing or not as good. And I remember saying to you, "I have tried to write, and I just can't do it." And I remember you just looked at me and said, "Well, maybe you're not supposed to." I thought, *Really? I don't have to?* You won't even remember that you said that; it just came out of your mouth. You were saying, *I hear you have great gifts speaking to the youth, and you really communicate to them, and so keep doing that.* It was like you were saying you were okay with me and that I had something to offer even though I was not at your level. You used what knowledge you had to build me up, to lift me up, to edify me. And there were other men that came into my life who did the same thing and helped me in some of my shortcomings, and I actually began to feel like I had something to offer. They said to me, "Why don't you help me in communicating, because every time I talk, people sleep." I was amazed that I could help them.

It happened again today at lunch when we were praying over John and someone was thanking God for him, saying, *I love you more, God, because of John and his writings and teachings.* That is true for me too: I love Jesus more because of John.

Not to embarrass you, John, but it was your writings that I would read—and they were deep and they were rich—and I walked away more in love with Jesus. And it just gave me this confidence about using the mind to stir the affections. I want to do that with other young people. And we are seeing how there are so many younger people now that are getting it and understanding things and understanding some of these concepts, and it is causing them to love Jesus more. Not puff them up but really cause them to fall more in love with Jesus. And I want to thank you, John, because I do feel like I love Jesus more because of your writings and your thinking. I love people more because of your writing. The main thing—I think my wife can attest to this—is that I enjoy God more. I do. I love knowing him. And some of that was gone for a while for me. There was still that underlying fear, still that respect for God, still a lot of these things that showed reverence toward the Lord, but it was through John's writings that I began enjoying God again. I began really desiring him again.

So it was thinking that made me love God. And so when I saw

that could happen, it made me more and more excited to read more, to study more, and to encourage other people to do the same.

John, there is the possibility that with our thinking, we produce more distinctions from and differences with others. And yet the apostle Paul charges literally "to think the same thing," several times in Philippians and in a few other places. He encourages us toward thinking and toward unity at the same time. How does the life of the mind relate to greater unity rather than only to greater diversity in the church?

JOHN PIPER: You are absolutely right that a devotion to doctrine, and especially thinking hard about doctrine, causes one to define it, and as soon as you define that it is this and not this, this and not this, the not-this believers are now not believing what you believe, and there are tensions. And the more important the issue is, the greater the tensions, and none of us likes that kind of tension.

The first thing I would say exegetically is that the word group Paul uses there is not the *neō* word group but the *phroneō* word group. . . .

AL MOHLER: He was not a scholar there, by the way.

JOHN PIPER: . . . The command to "be minded," to think a certain way—in general those commands are a word group in Greek that's very difficult to bring over into English. "Attitude" would be as good a translation as "think." *Have the same attitude*, Paul is saying. "Let this mind be in you which is also in Christ Jesus" doesn't mean in that case, even though it should be, that we are thinking his thoughts about biology or thoughts about the cross. It means he emptied himself, took the form of a servant, so *have a servant mind*. And so usually the call to "have one mind" is the call to have one orientation on humbling yourself to be a servant. But that does not answer the problem. There is more to say.

The apostle Paul really does want us to think the same thoughts doctrinally. He is not into, "Hey, have a couple of views about the cross, the more the better"—that is not the way Paul would think at all. He would like there to be one pervasive understanding of the atonement in this room and around the world, and so the command,

I think, means "work at it." And the way to work at that is not to say it doesn't matter.

When the command comes, "Have the same mind," or "Think the same thing," then what do you do? Well, you preach and you write as persuasively as you can and as kindly and as winsomely and as lovingly as you can. And when there is a pocket in your church that is swarming in a little clique, getting a little different view about something, you don't take angular potshots at them from the pulpit. You call them up and say, "Can I come meet with your group?" You say, "Tell me what you're thinking. Where did this come from? Can I give you some reasons why this doesn't look right to me?" And so an effort is made. So the whole constellation of reconciliation commands—"love your enemy" and "be slow to anger" and "be quick to listen"—all those things that we usually think of only in terms of relational dynamics—they are all intellectual dynamics as well. And we would do better, probably, in the evangelical world if there were more phone calls. Wouldn't we? Fewer blogs, more phone calls.

Now I am not one of those who says you cannot criticize somebody publicly until you have called him on the phone. I don't think you have to necessarily call first if he has been public in espousing an error. But there are a lot of cases when you can call. And that might go a long way toward rectifying things. I write more letters to the editor with a note at the top, *This is not for publication*, than I do for publication. I gave up on writing letters to editors years ago—but I still write to an editor when I am steaming about something and say, "Look, I am upset with what you did. I don't want the world to know that; I just want you to know that. Why in the world would you publish such an article?" Or something like that.

So I think the two responses I have are, one, those verbs are generally attitudinal. But, two, we should work toward thinking the same about doctrinal issues, and the best way is to teach and preach and speak in winsome, loving, and compelling ways.

AL MOHLER: What John just did for us, what he just modeled there, is actually thinking about thinking. What he just did was say, "Look, in order to understand the question just asked of me, we need to go back to the text and understand it is not quite so simple as you just presented it" (which was great the way that you set that up and laid it out).

And I think John is exactly right. We Christians are the truth people. We cannot act like truth does not matter. And the more we talk about truth, the greater the risk is that we are going to disagree, or we are going to find that there is a miscommunication, or we are going to have to work things out. That is the price we are going to pay till Jesus comes, because the price of not doing that is turning ourselves into a nonthinking, nontheological, nondoctrinal people who will lose the gospel. So we must be unapologetic about it, but it is going to humble us for a number of reasons. Because in the give-and-take of this conversation in the believing church (I don't mean with unbelievers and with liberal theologians and skeptics and all the rest), we are going to find ourselves in error. We are going to need a lot of Priscillas and Aquilas to take a lot of Apolloses aside and say, "That wasn't right."

I recently preached a message in chapel where I told about a time when I was in error and desperately needed Priscilla and Aquila to show up and correct me. It turned out his name was Carl Henry—so it was not Priscilla. But it was Aquila who showed up in this case to fulfill that function, and I needed the correction. It has happened more times than I am even aware of, where I have been corrected by the preaching of God's Word.

We have to risk disagreement. Disagreement is not the worst thing. Disagreement is the price you pay to make sure you actually know what you are talking about and clarify what you are saying. And you can be in relationships where you love each other all the more for it. I have Christian brothers who will challenge me and whom I challenge, and at the end of it, we worship God more faithfully together because of this.

Also, disagreement gives us the chance to think out loud. One of the gifts we need to give each other is to expose our thinking to each other. We tend in our intellectual narcissism, and I'm as guilty of this as anyone else, to want to show up with a finished product. "Here's my position. I have arrived here." But we need to be vulnerable, because we will be far more faithful if we will line out our thinking so that we can watch each other think, hear each other think, and say, "If that's not tightened back here, you're going to end up over here," or, "I don't think you heard what you said when you were there."

We need to have the maturity and the discernment to say there are some things we have to be united on or we cannot recognize each other as brothers and sisters in Christ. Someone asked me a question one time: "What do you say to someone," a believer, I was told, "who doesn't believe in the bodily resurrection of Christ?" Here's what you are: not a believer. We have a category problem there. There are certain things that have to be believed. And this is a New Testament issue—the apostles had to say here is what the gospel is. You have to know this much. Romans 10, for example. They have a very clear example. If you're not there, you're not a believer. You're not a Christian. You are not inside. You're still outside. But why don't you get inside?

There is a second level, I suggest, in which we have some serious disagreements. And it's not because we don't love the Lord and we don't love the Bible and we don't want to serve Jesus. But there are issues that divide us denominationally that aren't accidents. They go back to serious disagreements about things that matter, and we love the Lord and we love the truth enough to know they really matter. We might both be wrong, but we can't both be right. But we do recognize each other as sincere believers in Christ, and we can witness together. Whitfield and Wesley could share the gospel together and preach together and be involved in ministry together. We can be in this room together. We can exalt in Christ together. And we know that the commonalities that bring us here are why we're here, but we're still who we are. We walk in the door; we didn't become Desiring-God robots. We are who we are, and until Jesus comes back, we will have to work with some things. And in humility there are going to be some things we disagree about until our Lord Teacher corrects his church and purifies and sanctifies his church in common.

But then there's a third category, and this is important for us, too. There are things we disagree about that don't matter to the preaching and teaching of the gospel or the right ordering of the church. There may be as many positions on some questions of eschatology as there are people in this room, and I can live with that so long as we're absolutely certain of the coming visible, triumphant return of the Lord Jesus Christ to cleanse and claim his church and the consummation of all things according to everything that Scripture proclaims. There could be all kinds of different positions on how the human soul originates and this or that and different interpretations of things that don't matter, and we recognize that. In humility we need to recognize that's just another sense of our fallenness. That's another sign of our incomplete sanctification. We can still worship together and work together, and we can agree on the ordering of the church on these things together.

So that requires some maturity. If you make a third-order issue a first-order issue, you're going to blow the place up. If you make a first-order issue a third-order issue, you're going to flush the gospel. It requires some maturity and growing up. And we need to do it together. So think out loud.

John, would you close us in prayer?

JOHN PIPER: *Father in heaven, we ask that you would become more and more our teacher. We love that phrase of Paul's to the Thessalonians, that they are "God-taught to love one another." We believe that you have ordained to do it through your inspired Word and often through anointed pastors and teachers and small-group leaders. Whatever avenues, Lord, we want to be God taught. We want to know things, feel things, and do things according to reality—yourself, your Son, your ways. So let this conference, oh God, have that effect increasingly on our souls. Make us a God-taught people for the sake of this world that needs the light of the church and the salt of the church everywhere. I pray this in Jesus's name.*
Amen

Acknowledgments

We thank God for Rick Warren, R. C. Sproul, Al Mohler, Thabiti Anyabwile, and Francis Chan, who not only participated in the conference in October of 2010 but also gave the extra time to revise and expand their messages into the preceding chapters. The partnership in the gospel we share with these five brothers is rich and a gift beyond words. Thank God for such dear comrades in the Cause.

We thank God for Lane Dennis, Justin Taylor, Lydia Brownback, and the many at Crossway who now have partnered with us for eight volumes growing out of the annual Desiring God National Conference each fall. We are increasingly grateful for the profound theological and ministry partnership we share with the team at Crossway.

We thank God for Jon Bloom, Scott Anderson, and the team at Desiring God who invest countless hours in planning and executing both the fall conference and the winter conference for pastors.

We thank God for Nathan Miller, who has partnered with us in this ministry for over four years while completing his seminary studies. His joyful service and knack for anticipating needs before they arise have been a significant manifestation of grace to us.

We thank God for Bethlehem, her support, and the leadership of her council of forty elders. May God grant that her love and mission and service in the Twin Cities continue to increase. Let's keep torching the glacier.

We thank God for the unique strength and joy he gives through our wives, and children still in the house—for John, Noël and Talitha; for David, Megan and Carson and Cole.

Finally, and most significantly, we thank God for Jesus, who "loved us and gave himself up for us" (Eph. 5:2). Not only has God demonstrated "his love for us in that while we were still sinners,

Christ died for us" (Rom. 5:8)—unspeakably and eternally precious—but he also has given the Spirit of Jesus to us and the other contributors (and all those in Jesus). All good in this volume is ultimately owning to the Giver of "every good gift and every perfect gift" (James 1:17). The errors, oversights, and overstatements are ours.

May the person and work of Jesus be more engaged by minds, treasured by hearts, and displayed by hands because of this book. May Jesus Christ be praised.

David Mathis
Twin Cities, Minnesota
Cinco de Mayo, 2011

Subject Index

adorakia (Gk. freedom from oppression and anxiety), 74
aichmalōtizō (Gk. to control, to conquer, to bring into submission), 26
anti-intellectualism, 15–16
archae (Gk. chief principle), 69
asunetos (Gk. foolish), 123
authenticity, 28–29

being intellectually stretched, 138–39
belief, operating conditions of, 62
big bang theory, 70
boasting in the Lord, 118, 141–42
body of Christ, 137–38

character, 38–39
Christian community, 14
conscience, 52–53
conviction, 37–38
cosmos, 69

diephtharmenōn (Greek: depraved), 123
disagreement, 151–53
disciple, as "learner," 32
diversity. *See* pluralism
"doers" (hands), 19
doing, importance and limits of, 17–18

dreaming great dreams, 42–43

emaraiōthēsan (Greek: futile), 123
Enlightenment, the, 49
Epicureans, 74–75
epōrōthē (Greek: hardened), 123
evangelicalism, Bebbington's distinctives of (biblicism; conversionism; crucicentrism; activism), 47
evangelism, 58–59
faithfulness, 30; as purifying discipline, 12n1

fall, the, 54–55; consequences of, 54; the Reformers' view of, 55; the Roman Catholic Church's view of, 55. *See also* fall, the, noetic effects of
fall, the, noetic effects of, 54–58; distractedness, 56; dogmatism and closed-mindedness, 57; failure to draw the right conclusion, 57; faulty perspective, 57; forgetfulness, 56; ignorance, 56; inconsistencies, 57; intellectual apathy, 57; intellectual fatigue, 57; intellectual pride, 57–58; miscommunications, 58; partial knowledge, 58; preju-

Name Index

Scripture Index

⁂ desiringGod

If you would like to explore further the vision of God and life presented in this book, we at Desiring God would love to serve you. We have thousands of resources to help you grow in your passion for Jesus Christ and help you spread that passion to others. At our website, www.desiringGod.org, you'll find almost everything John Piper has written and preached, including more than forty books. We've made over thirty years of his sermons available free online for you to read, listen to, download, and in some cases watch.

In addition, you can access hundreds of articles, find out where John Piper is speaking, learn about our conferences, and browse our online store. John Piper receives no royalties from the books he writes and no compensation from Desiring God. The funds are all reinvested into our gospel-spreading efforts. Desiring God also has a whatever-you-can-afford policy, designed for individuals with limited discretionary funds. If you'd like more information about this policy, please contact us at the address or phone number below. We exist to help you treasure Jesus Christ and his gospel above all things because he is most glorified in you when you are most satisfied in him. Let us know how we can serve you!

Desiring God
Post Office Box 2901 Minneapolis, Minnesota 55402
888.346.4700   mail@desiringGod.org

PASTOR -
JOHN PIPER 612 338-7653
BETHLE HEM BAPTIST CHURCH.

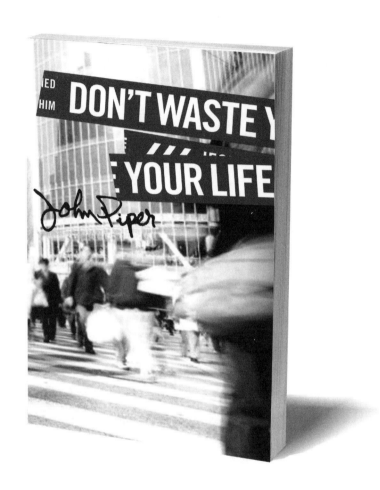

MAKING OUR LIVES COUNT FOR ETERNITY

"God created us to live with a single passion to joyfully display his supreme excellence in all the spheres of life. The wasted life is the life without this passion. God calls us to pray and think and dream and plan and work not to be made much of, but to make much of him in every part of our lives."

The Life of the Mind
and the Love of God

"This book is a plea to embrace serious thinking as a means of loving God and people. It is a plea to reject *either-or* thinking when it comes to head and heart, thinking and feeling, reason and faith, theology and doxology, mental labor and the ministry of love. It is a plea to see thinking as a necessary, God-ordained means of knowing God. Thinking is one of the important ways that we put the fuel of knowledge on the fires of worship and service to the world."

—*From the Introduction*